Birds and Light

Lars Jonsson

Birds and Light

PRINCETON UNIVERSITY PRESS

PRINCETON AND OXFORD

If reality is not sufficient, one should lay down the brush,
otherwise there will be too much ornamental beauty.
Reality means substance and body,
ornamental beauty is gracefulness;
substance and body originate from nature,
ornamental beauty and
gracefulness from the works of man.

HAN CHO 1121

Published in the United States, Canada, and the Philippine Islands by Princeton
University Press, 41 William Street, Princeton, New Jersey 08540

In the United Kingdom and European Union, published by Christopher Helm,
an imprint of A & C Black (Publishers) Ltd., 37 Soho Square, London W1D 3QZ

First published in Swedish by Bokförlaget Atlantis AB, Stockholm

ISBN 0-691-11489-7

Library of Congress Control Number 2002111132

This book has been designed by Christer Jonson.
The typeface is Indigo Antiqua, designed by Johan Ström in 1999.
The paper used in the book is yellow-tinted Lessebo Linné from Lessebo Bruk
of Klippan, Sweden, and PhoeniXmotion Xenon from Scheufelen in Germany,
and weighs 150 g.
Reproduction, printing, and binding have been carried out by
Graphicom Srl of Vicenza, Italy.
The work was completed in September 2002.

Translated and edited by
David A. Christie and Erik Hirschfeld

www.pupress.princeton.edu

Printed in Italy 2002

1 3 5 7 9 10 8 6 4 2

Contents

There is an aesthetic convention that states that direct observation of nature is not sufficient for genuine artistic creativity. Monet painted with his eye, but what an eye! This is an often repeated cry in art literature. When it comes to such a master as Monet praise seems inevitable, but is visual genius enough? On the other hand, it has been said of Cézanne that he painted more with his brain than with his eye. There is a subtext here which implies that 'the eye's capacity for observation' is subordinate to the brain's 'higher' capacity. In any case, artistic activity is acknowledged as such through the fact that it is associated with advanced thinking. Simply receiving and spontaneously reproducing visual impressions can certainly be accepted as expression of the beauty of rapid inspiration. A greater thing, however, is to reflect depth of thought.

Nevertheless, something is not quite right here. The difference is not in fact a matter of visual receptiveness as opposed to a more advanced capacity for thought. The truth is that Monet did not paint with his eye – like Cézanne, he painted with his brain. It need hardly be said that perception is a cohesive but at the same time complex process adapted for interpretation and understanding.

A consciousness of the physiology of perception teaches us to avoid hasty assertions on artistic intelligence. What seems to be an expression of 'the eye's genius' does not necessarily mean a lack of dimension in depth. What can put obstacles in the way is – as initially intimated – the long-established notion of the supremacy of abstraction. The idea is that that which is too close to the direct representation or the obviously illusory is not sufficiently noble to be taken seriously as part of what is artistically respectable. Aesthetic conventions, however, are impermanent in their nature. We know only too well that values change. In the light of a positive view of nature, the concentrated observation of wildlife also opens up a pathway to a free aesthetic discourse which develops along its own lines without major programmatic gestures.

How remarkable it is to imagine how the reflected or the already diffracted light is captured and ingeniously arranged by our visual system, which makes perceptible the forms of creatures in the world around us! Through the eye's miraculously elastic optics the radiation of light from the world outside places an upside-down picture on the retina, from where the optic nerve sends impulses on to the visual centre to be adjusted and arranged in collaboration with other brain centres. The visual process is an adaptation to the dynamics of the world around us. The constantly oscillating eye sees only change in spatial or temporal frequencies. The physical space is in constant motion: light intensities rise and fall, shadows come and go; contrasts are created between the distinct and the indistinct; colour, size and shape change according to distance and angle of view. There is therefore a need for stabilisation in order to enable rapid detection of change and deviation, anticipation of patterns of movement and the maintaining of perceptual constancy whether it concerns colour, size, boundary lines, strength of light or movement. Connections exist here, where the brain's

7

different visual centres are in contact with other vital sensory functions such as hearing, touch, taste or smell, with the subconscious and with the limbic system's emotional response mechanisms.

The choice to observe and reproduce birds and the movement of birds demands a high activation of the motive powers of perception – visual acuity, sharp hearing, touch, alertness. This is obvious, but at the same time it presupposes a patiently acquired knowledge of species coupled with ecological knowledge, which in its aesthetic dimension turns into a profound respect for what is constituted by nature's lebensraum. The most difficult thing remains: to produce pictures of what is seen, to make relevant choices, to reduce the distance between the spontaneity of the visual impression and the expressiveness of the annotation of it.

The pictorial world which draws its inspiration from nature-observation is founded on a long tradition, which takes the form of a web of observation and elusive but ever-present experiences of beauty. Here, Lars Jonsson occupies a far advanced position by virtue of a rare combination of ornithological knowledge and a highly developed capacity for remoulding visual impressions in water-colour and oil, the media of the old masters. Here we find a creative interaction between the experiences drawn from practised watching and the artistic shaping of the subject.

His search for knowledge has patiently followed empirical paths. Systematic studies of bird species in Sweden and on long trips in Europe, the Middle East,

Siberia and North America have sharpened his eye to the possibilities of the bird picture. He also finds other routes to partial understanding. The prepared bird in museum collections provides the opportunity for close study, while the recently dead bird serves as a better memento of the vitality of the plumage, the arrested movement represented by the arrival of death. The photographic picture, too, provides him with information, albeit more as an aid to memory.

Finally, the personal observation is the focal point. It is a matter of capturing the passing moment. The movement of light and colour which is played out in brief spaces of time is a question of perceptual reconstruction, of memory and expectations. Lars Jonsson, in his bird pictures, has transformed his visual powers into a euphoriant virtuosity in which there seem to be no delays between impulse and the movements of the hand. Following old and tested paths, he puts his trust in the observer's ability to detect and ponder over the precision of what is not distinctly stated. Richness of detail will not do; the truth must be conjured up through lack of sharpness, through a rapidly adopted posture, through what is not stated clearly. Truth is found in the bird's evasive character which it reveals in quick encounters, in the transition from the clearly marked bulk to the dissolving of the apparentness of the bodily form.

The transparency of the water-colour makes it particularly suitable for the 'intrinsic poetry of observation', which constitutes the essence of Lars Jonsson's artistry. The rapid hand, the fluidness, the pigments applied by water to the absorbent paper give a light which expresses the air and the thematic nature of light in a way that is true to the spirit of reality.

Spatial distance provides room for thought. What happens when what is in the distance comes to meet us with a strong but unconscious presence? When Lars Jonsson with the help of the telescope studies the individual bird, the ingrained picture gets displaced. It is not a confrontation, an expression of nature's struggle for existence. He allows us, as privileged observers, to take part in a brief process, a contemplative moment. We encounter a world where the existential questions temporarily step aside before the miracle of perception.

The kingfishers' most propitious times occur the week before and the week after the winter solstice, as in the eastern Mediterranean Sea this can often be a period of calm weather. The period is known as the halcyon days after the queen Halkyone, transformed by the gods into a kingfisher so that she would forevermore delight in life over the open water. Pictured here is a place of tranquillity and timelessness which also embraces Lars Jonsson's landscape, even if the kingfisher of mythology has taken on the shape of an Avocet.

HANS HENRIK BRUMMER

Head Curator, National Museum
Prins Eugens Waldemarsudde

The Hooded Crow was the first of his birds that stopped me in my tracks (and still does so – I find it difficult to tear myself away from crows). That was 25 years ago, when I had obtained the first volume of what was to become his five-volume series of guides, *Fåglar i naturen* (1976-80). The first one dealt with the habitats 'woods, parks and gardens', those inland places where I happen to live (spruce forest, low mountains, old watercourses since converted into fields and pasture), and where I still carry out my basic ornithological observations. The crow is there on the page of the book, and it is defiant. Its posture is different from the usual one shown in field guides. This crow has its body turned slightly away from us, with its back more or less facing the observer, but it is twisting its head and looking 'disdainfully' over its shoulder; it has just opened its bill, and it is defying us.

Even lousy ornithologists like myself know what a crow looks like. We seldom mistake it in the field, and we do not need pictures in field guides. But crows are also in the guides, and they have to be, of course: the principle of the field guide is not exclusion, but completeness. So, how does one paint a picture that nobody really 'needs'? This is the question that Lars Jonsson appeared to have asked himself with his crow, and his answer seems to have been to paint a picture of the bird's character, or its attitude. Or, quite simply, what it says to us.

In other words, not just what the crow 'looks like', but how it feels to see it, how it addresses us.

But address? The bird should address us?

Much of the rich mythology surrounding common (and some uncommon) bird species has arisen from something that has to do with 'being spoken to', our experience of encounters with them. In field guides, with their requirement for correctness, such a thing as 'addressing the observer' may well be deemed to be highly unscientific, and I am not sure that that is a term that can be applied to Lars Jonsson. Or else 'being addressed' amounts to no more than another way of looking at things, even in the field: identifying a bird by the feeling that it awakens in the observer – 'by feel'. Looking at birds in this way is not necessarily more approximate, more arbitrary, than methods based on exact assessment. Perhaps even highly skilled ornithologists sometimes use 'feel' when identifying certain species – whether the bird 'feels' bigger or smaller, how its flight 'feels', and so on. Similarly, when it comes to identifying the songs of some warblers, it is the song's character, rather than specific sounds, that we have to go by.

Whatever the case, I had leafed through field guides where the birds were portrayed with great accuracy and precision, but the illustrations nevertheless did not really show what the birds 'looked like', what it was like to encounter them; the pictures made no attempt to capture the relationship between the bird and its observer. And that was what was so astonishing about Lars Jonsson's crow, the fact that he had incorporated the human element into his field-guide illustration, man's feeling when faced with the crow, the bird which, after all, nobody ever misidentifies (under reasonable conditions). The Hooded Crow is one of those birds which we do not need to check in the bird guides, yet I still return to Lars Jonsson's picture, over and over again. It is an encounter, or a work of art.

Of course, this applies equally to other species in his field-guide series. I have myself developed an attachment to his Oystercatcher, his Woodcock, his Blackbird … certainly. To be honest, it has to be said that he has substituted several of these pictures in his second ornithological work, *Birds of Europe with North Africa and the Middle East* (1992), maybe because he thought that the 'human element' in them had been overdone.

It was a delight when the new volumes arrived, 'sea and coast', 'lake, river, marsh and field', 'mountain regions' … like instalments in an epic tale. It took four years for the work to be completed. I had long regarded Erik Rosenberg's *Fåglar i Sverige* as something more than a field guide, more as a collection of poems, for the poetic quality of the species descriptions. Now, here was a series of new Swedish field guides in which the pictures had a similarly poetic quality. These were books to peruse not just for practical purposes, but for something more difficult to define, perhaps for exploring one's own feelings towards different bird species, the images of them within oneself – almost for a kind of self-knowledge.

The first time I came across the man himself was in autumn 1996, at a symposium arranged by the Vitterhetsakademi (the literary academy), dedicated to Bruno Liljefors and the traditions, and later documented in Hans Henrik Brummer's and Allan Ellenius's 1997 anthology *Naturen som livsrum: Ekologiska perspektiv i modern litteratur och bildkonst* [The countryside as a habitat: ecological perspectives in modern literature and art]. He began his talk with a somewhat dramatic statement: 'I'm good at birds, and I do not see that as a handicap.' While this may sound rather strange, his audience knew very well what he meant. His words were a retort directed at a debate over art that has been going on at least throughout the period known as modernism, and especially in Sweden, where wildlife painting (and literary portrayal of nature) has persistently been regarded with suspicion, or treated with condescension. Some have voiced the opinion that ornithological expertise of the kind demonstrated by Lars Jonsson should not be seen as an artistic resource. Specialist scientific knowledge was said to be the opposite of art's specific concept of knowledge; scientific precision would lead to artistic haziness. Furthermore, interest in the non-human (birds, other animals) was considered a lesser kind of ardour in the context of art, which ought to have higher objectives than the animal level. Such views have afflicted a number of outstanding portrayers of wildlife in both literature and pictorial art (photography and film) throughout virtually the whole of the twentieth century. In the annals of history, the portrayers of nature have generally been the material of footnotes or quite simply ignored, hushed up.

Nor has Lars Jonsson escaped in this respect, and at times he has lamented the fact, as in this reflection from *En dag i maj* [One day in May] (1990):

> When the Lapwing turns its back to me, the sun produces a dazzling violet reflection which matches the colour of the translucent early-purple orchids. To reproduce its back in water-colours I should doubtless have to splash on plenty of pure Winsor violet. Thoughts come to mind of Abbott Thayer; had he been alive now, he would have nodded approval at this approach. He was an American impressionist working during the later part of the 1800s and the beginning of the 1900s. Just before his discovery that birds' colour patterns were echoes of the environment in which they lived, all for the purpose of providing them with camouflage, he became so fixated by this thought that all of nature's creatures were incorporated into this pattern. In the history of art, he is mentioned as one of the most promising impressionists but who 'unfortunately' became too absorbed in investigating natural history.

This was the kind of empathy which he expressed when he began his talk in 1996. And his audience smiled wryly, mostly saddened by the fact that even one such as Lars Jonsson should feel somewhat oppressed by an attitude of art historians that ought to have been abandoned long ago. Afterwards we had lunch, and a casual conversation commenced which now forms the text of this book.

What is it that we see in nature? What do we discern, or take notice of? What is it that represents nature for us?

Species? Or individuals?

How we answer such questions is determined to some extent by how each of us sees himself or herself in regard to nature, in one's own eye. For a field-guide author, the question is a vital one. Lars Jonsson has answered it succinctly: the individual.

Is the comprehensive picture of a variable object more representative than one particular individual? Imagine having to draw a typical image of the royal family: should one individual be portrayed or the characters from several be combined? In the latter case, there is the risk that the outcome will be a pedagogic one, in other words a chart of characters enabling any one representative to be recognised. The result is an identification tool, but not a visual experience of what 'the royals' look like; it does not become a reality until one sees a real representative, i.e. a true individual (portrayed from life). It has little of the feeling which I am seeking to achieve.

This view of the individual factor certainly has to do with an experience of participation. In his wildlife books, Lars Jonsson sees himself as a part of the same great landscape, the same great moment, as that inhabited by the birds he paints: the time when the bird pauses (or forages, or busies itself with breeding duties), while he watches it in his telescope and struggles to capture it on water-colour paper, is a time which the artist and the bird share. Painting can come to be like a mutual bond between man and animal. Lars Jonsson's pictures are quite often profoundly serene: the tranquility of the resting birds is also his own, at the same time as he is carefully engaged in committing them to the sketchbook, capturing their markings, colours and volume … their essence. There is in his pictures a sense of relaxation which is bound up not only with technical virtuosity but just as much with a state of profound empathy, or perhaps we should call it 'contact with the bird within himself'. He seems to submit to and rejoice at this state of empathy, unreservedly, as a human capacity, a rich capability. This does not, of course, mean that he sentimentalises nature. Being part of it does not equate to the erasing of all boundaries between man and the surrounding environment. But all the while Lars Jonsson crosses the unnecessary boundaries, such as the uneasy borderline between 'observation' and 'experience'. Empathy and the unceasing scrutiny of the individual birds around him become both an ornithological and an artistic corrective: never believe that one has finished a species, even the 'common' ones. In the introduction to the first volume of *Fåglar i Naturen*, he expresses this attitude almost as a creed, or doctrine.

In recent years I have had innumerable opportunities – including from my workroom – to study House Sparrows and Chaffinches, two of the suburb's typical birds. One winter about 4 years ago, I decided to attempt to achieve a form of 'definitive' statement on the House Sparrow's colour, markings, shape and movements, in other words its general appearance. The birds are almost continuously present outside my window. I keep a sketchpad on the desk so that I can always make fresh sketches. To my surprise, however, I seem repeatedly to be finding new lines and shapes, new colours and patterns, new types of behaviour and posture, new angles of approach. Not even for such a well-known species as the House Sparrow can I manage to make a definitive image!

Even the House Sparrow could not be conclusively and ultimately defined in a picture. Having seen many of Lars Jonsson's bird portraits, we ought perhaps to treat his statement on the impossibility of the task with a degree of wonder, as a manifestation of extreme humility. In *Fåglar i Naturen*, however, he writes more about the importance of 'really looking at and listening to even the commonest species' – that we have never 'finished' with them, or rather with 'the capability for looking' at them. There is perhaps a kind of 'rationality' in his plea never to stop studying the common birds, those which are regularly present outside our window: by so doing, we can then exclude them before identifying a rarity. (Similar 'rational' suggestions are made, incidentally, by Erik Rosenberg in *Fåglar i Sverige*, on the Hooded Crow in particular: 'The prospective field ornithologist should become fully acquainted with the crow with regard to its behaviour, flight and vocalisations, for many dark birds are glimpsed in woodland and fields, and the crow can be present everywhere, but its distinctive grey and black plumage is by no means always visible.') For a birdwatcher with vague ambitions, the idea of getting to know a species so as to be able to discount it, to eliminate it, may seem somewhat offensive. But Lars Jonsson never stops at that level of 'rationality' (nor, of course, did Erik Rosenberg). For him, the various birds are instead 'inexhaustible', we cannot reach a total understanding or knowledge of them, he writes, nor of our own experience of them. Getting to know a bird is one thing, and not the same as knowing everything about it. Rather, the opposite is the case: only when we 'know' a bird species can we really begin to see it, to see individuals of the species, to meet the real living (not 'theoretical') creatures. Maybe Lars Jonsson's openness (or whatever we may call it) as an ornithologist is linked with the very fact that, as an artist, he has this particular eye – scrutinising instead of confirming. Anybody having such an eye is obviously richly endowed, being spared at least the tedium of seeing as a routine habit. Perhaps such an eye is even a kind of 'curse', never allowing its owner any peace? Perhaps it can never be content that everything looks 'normal', rather than being something to discover?

Never content with seeing just the species, and not always the individual? This is, in any case, what is so highly distinctive in his field guides. When he depicts a series of individuals, not some kind of abstract norm (which is a human notion, not an observation), he is of course offering us a fundamentally different perception of the world from that provided by generalisation. Lars Jonsson's bird-painting, both scientific and artistic, is really a meeting place of individuals, where the bird presents its character and the human being his insight.

Lars Jonsson lives in southern Gotland, near the sea, and has all kinds of white birds as his neighbours. This is no doubt one reason for his scientific interest in large gulls, such as the variations in their plumages, and the difficulties which they set the observer: 'I have always been fascinated by large gulls and their plumage development, partly because of the wide individual variation and partly because of the protracted period of development of the plumage.' In this connection, the way he sees things is not altogether uncontroversial, even though he is an international authority on the subject. And since it is a matter of 'one and the same' vision, irrespective of whether the resulting picture is called 'scientific' or 'artistic', we shall here dwell awhile on the scientific. In 1996, he wrote an article in the Swedish Ornithologists' Union's journal *Vår Fågelvärld* on the identification of the large gulls which have occurred in recent years in the Baltic Sea and on Gotland – 'yellow-legged gulls', which many of us no doubt refer to simply as 'Herring Gulls'. Science does not have a clear-cut, unequivocal species concept with which to work, but plays about with 'biological' or 'phylogenetic' species concepts in order to bring some sort of order to the complexity of forms in which life manifests itself. Where birds are concerned, there is the additional question of what one can actually see, in the field (or in real life), in terms of similarities and differences between different individuals. And this is Lars Jonsson's message in his article – the appearance of individual gulls on Gotland has caught his attention: 'For the last five years or so I have seen gulls which deviated from the *argentatus* pattern [Herring Gull] but which were left as "probably of eastern origin" and in some cases "probably adult *michahellis*".' He goes on to discuss whether an expansion into the Baltic Sea is taking place of gulls of a different kind from those we call Herring Gull, in fact of Yellow-legged Gulls birds originating from the Mediterranean or

Sketchbook: Lapwing
2nd February 2000
Water-colour 50x32 cm

The first Lapwing arrived unusually
early this year in association with a
warm period at the end of February.
Winter returned, however, at the
beginning of March, with below-zero
temperatures and snow for over a
week.

14

22.2.2000   09.45

southeast Europe, and which can be separated in the field. In the article, he presents his observations of these groups of birds (species? subspecies?), for which he suggests common names, reserving 'Yellow-legged Gull' for *Larus* [*cachinnans*] *michahellis* and proposing 'Caspian Gull' for *Larus* [*cachinnans*] *cachinnans*. He unravels subtle differences in various stages of the plumage development between the similar gulls which he has observed, and anybody – not just the ornithologist but also the artist – wishing to study more deeply the picture presented by Lars Jonsson may benefit by looking at a bit of his specialist prose. Here is an example, taken at random from the article:

> So far as I can see, *michahellis* never have a dark iris like *cachinnans*, but a pale one. In winter and spring they have an obviously intense yellow bill, often with a gull spot which 'bleeds over' onto the upper mandible, and an orange (more rarely, yellow) to red orbital ring. The structure recalls argentatus, but the bill is often characteristic because of the curvature of the upper mandible, which is often more marked. On juveniles with a black bill, the bill's shape is often quite different from that of *cachinnans* and *argentatus*. The head shape is otherwise like Herring Gull's, but the crown is often flatter, the forehead tends to be convex, and the junction between crown and nape is sharper, i.e. it looks more angular. The head appears relatively big, the body relatively short and heavy at the front but more tapered and 'slim' at the rear ... [and so on].

The article prompted some vehement reactions, but this is not the place to report on scientific debate. On the other hand, the text is of interest as a report on seeing, even if it is hard to keep up with its specific details. It sets out a number of characters relating to eye, bill and head of the Yellow-legged Gull *michahellis*, but these details have at the same time to be couched in linguistically vague terms, or reservations: 'often', 'more rarely', 'relatively' – 'flatter', 'sharper', 'more angular' ... in other words, these characters are such that they cannot be properly defined in language. Words are too imprecise to capture the nuances involved. But the eye can do so, writes Lars Jonsson. The eye, and therefore the picture. And it is here that his 'science' and his 'art' fuse together. Ornithologically, this way of seeing things is probably beyond many of us, but in art it is open and inviting. It requires that we discern, if not the species and the races perhaps, then the moments, the moods, the atmospheres ... in the landscapes that he paints, and the birds that inhabit those landscapes. Herein we also find his individuality as a 'bird artist', in the meditative observation, the profound restfulness in his vision.

The borderline between 'scientific' and 'artistic' animal-painting is sharp but not clear-cut. The tradition of scientific plates, which Lars Jonsson adopts in *Fåglar i Naturen* and *Birds of Europe*, has a long history,

with major landmarks in Sweden represented by such artists as Olof Rudbeck and the von Wright brothers (and in the USA, of course, by John James Audubon). Compared with depictions of animals in art from the same periods, these plates may appear 'dull' and 'unimaginative'. Their purpose was to reproduce the animal (the species) and its distinctive features as accurately as possible, as completely as if it were held in the hand. Artistic animal-painting was often of a different nature: it was full of human 'significance' – chases, pastorals, anecdotal encounters between animal and man ... which were not by any means necessarily without a delicate feeling for the animals portrayed. These two routes come together in Bruno Liljefors's great work – all his chase scenes (with and without the human ingredient), his ducks and geese in evening light, his intimate pictures at secluded bird nests, his birds migrating over open sea, and not least his 'studies of mimicry'. Liljefors's painting in his various periods had to endure the philosophical movements of the time. His animals have been looked at through the filters of ideology, but he himself never lost sight of a fundamental experience which he had as a child, and later expressed in *Det vildas rike*, in 1934 (and which Lars Jonsson particularly noted in his foreword to Martha Hill's 1987 book on Liljefors, *The Peerless Eye* (*Mästarens blick*):

> When I was very small – before I had been out of town – a farmer once came into our powder store with a brace of dead young Black Grouse which had perished during haymaking. I obtained them from him and for several days could not get them out of my mind, until I had to part with them. I was as if bewitched by the sight of their grey- and brown-vermiculated feathers. My previously ingrained ideas of which colours were attractive and which were not were turned upside-down when I beheld these wonderful combinations, which appeared as if deposited from the gloomy prehistoric era and told of the forest, the swamp, the moss on the boulders, the night sky between the branches. One could go on and on looking into this world, where there was no bottom or end but only an endless fountain of new discoveries.

Nowadays, the old zoological plates attract greater interest from art historians than from naturalists. Their poetic objectivity opens up routes for artistic reinterpretations. The hierarchical system remains, however, making a distinction between 'universal' art and 'partitioned' specialist illustration: the play of fictitious beetles by the painter and entomologist Karl Axel Pehrsson is taken with a different seriousness from that afforded to the entomologist and artist Björn Dal's pictures of real-life butterflies.

Lars Jonsson's drawings, those we can look at in his books, appear to be open to both factions, as much to the 'scientific' as to the 'artistic'. He has, like Bruno Liljefors, one eye, not two essentially different ones.

Faithfulness to nature is a difficult term, an exacting term. Faithfulness is an indivisible thing: one cannot be half-faithful – fidelity is absolute. Faithfulness to nature is a concept requiring truth.

But who is the person who looks at nature with fidelity? And from which viewpoint? Is the cave painter's faithfulness to nature identical to, say, the bird-photographer's?

Björn von Rosen, in his 1968 book *Om naturtrohet – och andra funderingar om konst* [On faithfulness to nature – and other thoughts about art], pondered over the way we relate to the animal pictures in the Lascaux caves. He dwells on the suggestion that the cave painters' pictures might be beyond our comprehension, that an unbridgeable gulf in time and in people's conception of the world divorces them from us, and that we must therefore be content to admire them from a distance, but can never get close to a real understanding of them. He writes:

I do not believe in that. All art is magic, all animal art has an element of invocation. Whether the artist starts his drawing in the conviction that it will bring luck with hunting or for joy at the intense animal spectacle witnessed a moment earlier is immaterial. Once he has got going, the magic has gripped him: the animal's breath envelops him, its scent is in his nostrils, he tries to catch its fleeing contours, he feels the roughness of the hair, the sharpness of the claws, the rhythm of its bolting escape. Later, when he wakes up, he may find that he can still see before him, on the paper or canvas, something of his vision: an outline of the bolting animal, a colour tint from the shaggy hair or the down. After such an experience he will not be so sure of the unbridgeability of the gulf, of the absence of all lineal communications, between him and his rock-carving ancestors.

Björn von Rosen, just like Liljefors before him, had also experienced a condescending attitude by his contemporaries towards animal painting. He upheld the integrity and value of the art form, not just against its antagonists but equally against its charlatans. Moreover, the concept of 'faithfulness to nature' was central for him:

What is faithfulness to nature? It is not something as simple as photographic exactness, 'zoology'. (Not art but zoology was the accusation often levelled at animal painting, which was regarded as too closely depictive, too 'true to nature'.)

I do not believe that any art, in painting or in literature, can be too true to nature. But it can be, and often is, true to nature in the wrong way, in other words false, listless, circumstantial, irresolute.

What Lars Jonsson wrote about cave painters, in his fundamentally important essay 'Ateljé i det fria' [Open-air studio] (*in Naturen som livsrum: Ekologiska perspektiv i modern litteratur och bildkonst*), sounds like a response to Björn von Rosen's reflections:

The powerful thing in the Paleolithic cave paintings is the sense of close proximity and empathy, of knowledge and of total presence, the capacity for extracting the important lines which distinguish one animal from another, which sum up the character, and do not allow the whole to be lost in the detail. They are not, of course, painted directly from life, but they are painted and carved from direct impressions of life, they reflect the artist-depicter's loaded relationship with the life encompassed in the animal's form. They transmit total presence, and to my mind many of the pictures in the newly discovered Chauvet caves communicate something personal right down through thirty thousand years of European culture.

These points of view are virtually identical, but perhaps we can also detect a difference, a time lapse between von Rosen and Lars Jonsson. Björn von Rosen was an artist (author) and a hunter. He had, in a way, a direct link with a view of animals which had continued unbroken since the time of the cave painters – a view of animals which combines distance in the field and inquisitive study of the grounded quarry … and where the 'bolting escape' of which he talks is an accepted condition. The relationship between hunter and animal, that which bridges the distance between them, is as much the rock, the spear, the arrow and the bullet … as the eye.

An upheaval came about when the weapon was replaced by other 'hunting equipment', by the camera and, later, the telescope.

In Sweden, the photograph was first used for the portrayal of nature in the early twentieth century, with Paul Rosenius and, especially, Bengt Berg, who became renowned far beyond the country's borders. And photography brought with it a change in the wildlife artist's position in the landscape: from having been a wandering undercover observer, he became a stationary and invisible watcher. Photographic apparatus and glass plates were far too cumbersome to haul around, so the 'camera hunter' had to install himself in camouflaged hides, set up in places where animals could be expected to reveal themselves often enough to allow them to be photographed   new types of station were sought for 'hunting'. This was a major reason why both Rosenius and Bengt Berg became bird-photographers, and why they came to specialise in nest photography (Paul Rosenius's greatest work is *Sveriges fåglar och fågelbon*, 1913-54). The birds put up with some disturbance at the nest: they returned to incubate eggs and brood chicks, even if hides suddenly appeared next to them and a shiny lens was pointed at them, accom-panied by intrusive shutter sounds. The photographer could rely on his birds.

And observation itself changed.

The new wildlife-portrayers cut themselves off from the world around them, shut out most of it, apart from what could be glimpsed through the narrow aperture where the camera was placed. Their activity became that of waiting.

Sketchbook: Studies of Siberian Gull
Bahrain, 7th February 1998
Pencil drawing 50x32 cm

During three trips to Bahrain in
1995–98 I studied the appearance, age
development and moult of Asiatic
large-gull populations which wintered
in the area, mainly Siberian Gull *Larus
heuglini heuglini* and Steppe Gull *Larus
(heuglini) barabensis*. I studied groups
of resting gulls and made notes and
sketches on their age, appearance and
state of moult. All individuals were
given a number, and data on them has
been entered in an excel programme
for statistical analysis. The figures in
the small square box are their moult
scores on a scale of one to fifty.

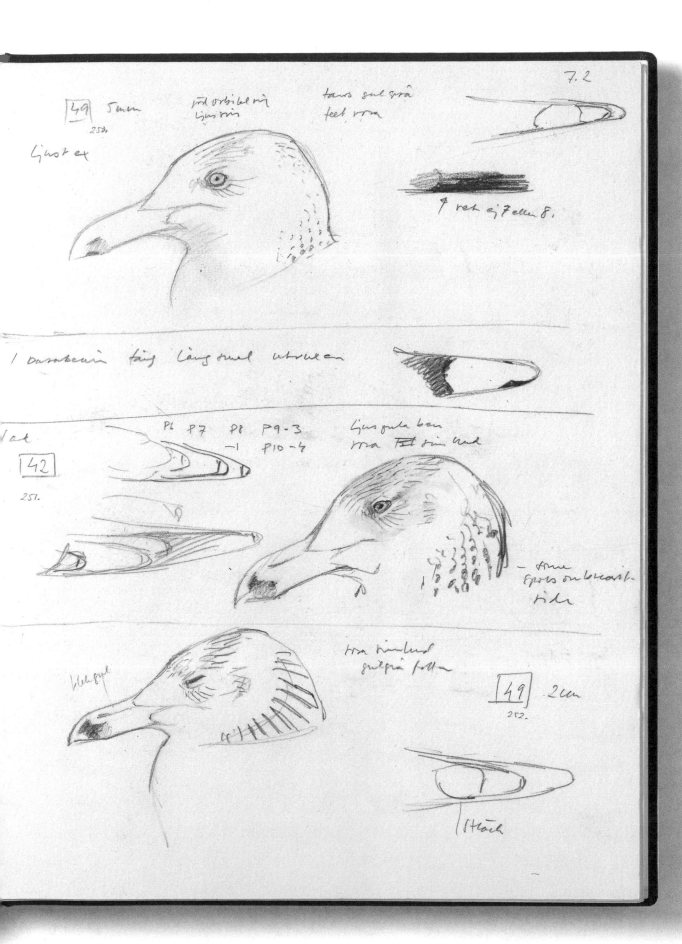

Sketchbook: Studies of Siberian Gull
in winter plumage, Bahrain,
7th February 1998
Pencil and water-colour 50x32 cm

Left: upper two birds probably in
their fourth calendar-year, i.e. in their
third winter, the lowest an adult bird
in winter plumage.
Right: at top a bird in its third
calendar-year, below an individual
probably in its fourth.

50
252.

3k

+ 1 50 und 3k
250.
sprächlig släuchn + säg en ließ mit Arthur senane

7.2. Very whiteheaded

vcrre 45/46 251

4 cal gen ?

typical pattern

The following scene is typical of bird-photographers' accounts, taken from Bengt Berg's *Tåkern: En bok om fåglarnas sjö* (1913). He had concealed himself in a flat-bottomed boat covered over with old withered reeds in order to take pictures of a Reed Warbler's nest. The birds around him are aroused, a Coot takes flight with its squeaking young ... and not least agitated is the female Reed Warbler, who gives a harsh alarm, but cannot bring herself to abandon the nest:

The Reed Warbler scrutinises the boat. Nothing is moving there. Just a single large glistening eye looks at her from the wilted heap of reeds, but it could just as well be a patch of water reflecting the light. The chicks, which have noticed her, stretch over the rim of the nest and one even opens its bill in expectation. The female becomes calmer, and as she slowly creeps around the boat she snaps up one insect after another. Her harsh calls have ceased, but her eye does not leave the shining object in the reed pile until the male arrives. He is strangely unconcerned and, although he has a bill full of mayflies and small flukes, he cannot forget the peeping of the young Coots but mimics them and chirps incessantly. He looks for a moment at the female's posture. She is giving no warning of anything, but he sees that she is a little uncertain. All her feathers are tightly sleeked, as if she were alarmed. The male raises his crown feathers – there is a hint of suspicion here and a touch of anger. But then a faint sound is heard from the nest and with a couple of hops he is up perched across a reed stem, where he can get to distributing his crop of orthopterans equally into the gaping yellow mouths. Then the female also dismisses her suspicions. Side by side the two co-operate in satisfying their chicks's demands, and long after the young have closed their sated bills the female is still sitting on the nest, quietly pondering over the shining patch in the heap of reeds. But the male, who sneaked away like a ghost as soon as his bill was empty, continues to try out all conceivable ways of imitating a young Coot.

Bengt Berg got close to the birds in a way that was different from that of the hunter-naturalists who had preceded him. His photographs have an intimacy which had never before been seen. The birds in his pictures appear unconcerned about his presence, as if he did not exist, and the photographs provide a glimpse into what was until then the unseen, secret corners in nature, which moreover, with new printing techniques, could now be circulated to large numbers of observers. Of course, we know that he could choose to dispose of plates which showed frightened birds, fleeing birds, and one can only guess at how many breeding attempts have been wrecked by his photo-pursuits and those of others. But this new method of depicting nature had a further import: it encouraged respect for wildlife. The portrayer of nature no longer killed the animals which he was to depict; he could (at least in principle) leave the wildlife unmolested.

With Bengt Berg, the opportunity led to this intimacy, or simply 'friendship' between man and wild animal, an idea (or utopian concept) which he came to realise in *Min vän fjällpiparen* (1917). This is when he finds a Dotterel's nest on open heathland on the mountain of Pidjastjåkko, 'south of Laukodalen, two days' journey east from Kebnekaise', and slowly gains the Lahol's (the Dotterel's Lapp name) 'trust' ... until the bird finally settles down to incubate its eggs in the palm of his hand.

At what point the change happened I really do not know, but now he harboured no more doubts. He came slowly forwards and climbed on to my hand. He went straight out again. There was something with which he was not happy. For a moment I feared that he would go away, but it was just that I did not understand him. He walked around my hand and looked at the eggs. He was not quite content with the way they were placed – who could know exactly how he would want them – and so he rolled and turned them with his bill until they were in the right position, as birds are in the habit of doing. Then he climbed confidently on to my hand and settled. Using his bill, he changed the odd blade of grass of which he did not approve. And then he sat again and looked innocently up at my face.

Little Lahol! – How little he suspected what joy he brought a human being. For had it been granted to me earlier to find the way to approach more timid birds and conquer their fear with cunning, then surely none would have made me so thankful for one of life's best moments as the little bird here on the mountain.

How long I spent with the Dotterel that day I do not know. My notebook was back in my coat pocket by the fire and I have to trust my memory.

So far as was possible, without disturbing the bird, I had crouched over a boulder by the side of the nest, and there I lay for a long time just looking at him.

The mountain terrain around us was bathed in the glorious warmth of the summer's day, and in my hand the little bird confidently incubated its eggs, just as I had dreamed and wished that he would. Through the greenery in my hand I could feel his heart beating.

The dream of a pact with the wild animal goes back a long way in man's history, and it is to some extent, of course, that dream to which Bengt Berg is referring. But his idea has been born just as much out of experiences from nest photography, the closeness to the breeding birds, their naturalness in front of the photographer. At any rate, the photograph (and shortly thereafter the ciné film) meant new opportunities for depicting animals, and therefore new opportunities for entering into their lives.

The suspense of the waiting photographer is of a different nature from that of the hunter. This is simply because the animal does not die, but it carries on living even after the 'trigger' has been pressed. Perhaps we can say that the photographer's suspense is extended, to the point even that he becomes peculiarly absorbed, not just in the landscape but also in a kind of mental distraction or introspection. Anybody who sits concealed in a sealed hide is for long periods reduced to considering his own 'internal landscape', and the photograph seems to have led to the sharp borderline between man and animal – hunter and quarry – becoming more diffuse.

Bengt Berg's photographs (and his restless, blissful, petulant and uneven prose) were the start of a new genre in wildlife portrayal. The patterns for the photographic wildlife book, and the nature film, were in broad terms already set out in his work. His importance can hardly be overestimated. Even wildlife-portrayers who were later to pursue totally different scientific and artistic routes, such as Erik Rosenberg and Sven Rosendahl, started out by following in his footsteps, their photographic ambitions uncertain. He himself was to be 'forgotten', or to be suppressed from the nation's memory, after his pro-German stance before and during the Second World War. His books, however, possess the colour of his time, and they could hardly be considered as propaganda. But his fate possibly contributed to the ambiguous status of wildlife art in Sweden.

The camera, in other words the photograph and the film, was the new medium for wildlife portrayal. Lars Jonsson has placed emphasis on another 'technical' innovation as being of decisive importance: the transition from the binocular to the telescope. This, of course, is associated with the level of disturbance: the telescope allows him to observe birds at such great distance that he avoids disturbing them, and he does not need to conceal himself as Bengt Berg did. But it is just as much about having the hands free, to be able to train the telescope on a single individual bird or group of birds and study them, while at the same time the hands are at work with the sketchpad and the water-colours. In addition, the telescope allows him to take up a new 'position' in the landscape – a kind of amalgamation of the wandering marksman and the concealed photographer. It enables him actually to place himself in the landscape, in the whole landscape – just as the birds do. The shoreline meadows of Gotland provide a panoramic outlook over extensive areas, with wide views over land, sea and sky. He shares the landscape with the bird in the telescope's eyepiece – man and bird are part of the same whole, they merely indicate two different points in it. The border between them is 'open'.

The following lines from the first short essay in his book *Dagrar* [Daylights], published in 2000, describe the importance of the telescope in the landscape in which he lives and paints:

> The Gotland landscape, along with its grandeur, harbours a sense of intimacy: one can settle down anywhere and feel embraced by the close environment. These individual sections, or microlandscapes, often remain undetected until one's eye fixes on a detail and the perspective is transformed. In my case, it is often the birds that open my eyes to these close environments. Many of the visual sensations that are the basis of my pictures are perceived through the eyepiece of the telescope. In practice, the magnifying eye of the lens is a prerequisite for making close-up studies of birds in their natural environment without my presence disturbing them. I can watch a resting wader for longer, have time to depict its movements, see details in the plumage, paint minor nuances in colour tone and the diffractions of light. But another dimension also exists in this combination of closeness and distance. There is a special magic in being able to see into an animal's world, to transport one's own presence to somewhere outside oneself. An internal landscape then takes a hold in the real life I see before me, a landscape the borders of which are defined from within myself, and a landscape the topography of which is my senses which have taken up their abode there. A solitary Redshank on the shoreline, a pair of Eiders on a rock or a Black-throated Diver steering away in the mist convey landscapes of this kind.

What he is describing is a different kind of pact between man and nature (bird) from that in Bengt Berg's dream of the Dotterel. The frontier

23

Sketchbook: Study of preening
Avocet and Caspian Tern
Aurriv, 16th April 2001
Water-colour and pencil 50x32 cm

Aurriv is a small promontory south of
Faludden in southeast Gotland. From
there I can look out over the shallow
sea bay, which is my most important
workplace. The Avocet is very
common, and during the spring I also
regularly see a few Caspian Terns.

24

which is opened up between the watching human and the bird when 'the perspective is transformed' in the telescope opens up in turn a frontier within man, in his perception and identity – man is transported outside himself. But at the same time something else happens, a different kind of transport: man's 'internal landscape' moves out into the surrounding exterior and transfers its colours to it, or actually replaces it – without careful observation of the bird diminishing or being lost. This double transportation is so complicated, so 'magical' or 'existential', that Lars Jonsson is unable to describe it beyond this, up to the meeting between the external and the internal landscapes – and the amalgamation of the two in the figures of the birds ... the Redshank on the shoreline, the Eider pair on a rock, the Black-throated Diver steering away in the mist. In his observation of the birds there is a knowledge that has gone beyond ornithology, but ornithology, and bird-painting, provide him with a means of formulating this knowledge.

In 'Ateljé i det fria', he gives another account of these 'open frontiers':

Drawing and painting in the open countryside is for me both a kind of submission to nature, its laws and powers, and also a way of feeling part of it, of being present in this natural world. To draw or paint out in the open, free of all constraints, is to embark on a journey towards what I have come to call 'dissolving' ['upplösning', literally dissolving, dissolution, decomposition]. Perhaps it is some sort of longing for another world, or to be able, like the birds, to overturn the laws of gravity and escape from an earthly reality. This lightness, this ethereal state, can come about when I am intensely engrossed in painting a living bird, when I am in a sense 'dissolved' between what I am observing and what I am painting. A state in which everything feels 'self-evident'. This state does not require any deliberate pictorial knack or aesthetic attitudes, but is characterised by absence of deliberacy, interpretation and physical frictions.

Experiences such as these are probably recognisable to some of us. If you happen to live inland, just sit at the edge of a wood and sit there long enough and quietly enough to 'disappear', to be transformed into one stump among other stumps, lost in a kind of impersonal perception. It is a powerful and singular experience; something happens with one's ingrained identity, which does not seem quite the same afterwards ... and it can be difficult later on to say anything about that state, that 'knowledge'. What words are capable of conveying it, when language seems to have become silent within one?

That is where Lars Jonsson paints, in that state of 'dissolubility'. His pictures are more than portrayals of species and individual birds. They can be called internal pictures – emanating from the state where he is 'in a sense "dissolved" between what I am observing and what I am painting'. So we, too, can make sense of the invitation he places before us: to see them as pictures of the human factor.

That may sound easy, but it may also be very difficult.

Modern-day art urges us to look into many sides of the human identity, such as that which we call 'evil'. But when it comes to man's relationship with the rest of creation, something which Sven Rosendahl once referred to as 'our faunistic paths of relationship', people are often perplexed. It is sometimes said that this is due to urbanisation, that fewer and fewer of us come across animals in our everyday life, but the towns and cities, too, are full of birds, for anybody prepared to see them. Perhaps we feel rather uncomfortable in our relationship with the rest of the animal kingdom, and prefer to keep animals at just the right distance by adopting a 'scientific' attitude – we have learnt not to anthropomorphise them. But what Lars Jonsson portrays in his art, and in what he writes about it, has nothing to do with the anthropomorphising of birds, of course. It can perhaps be said that he 'anthropomorphises himself' in his pictures, that he makes huge demands on his capacity as a human being, by allowing himself to 'be dissolved' in his encounter with the birds – then we might call this magic or mystique, if we wish.

Be that as it may, Lars Jonsson's bird pictures are not of birds, no matter what scientific knowledge they incorporate. They are human expressions, human formulations of what he sees, what he perceives. His comments on the 1991 water-colour of Black-headed Gulls, 'Vila i upplösning' [Repose when mind dissolved], are a strange and beautiful blend of work description and poetry.

Faced with the bright evening water I am forced to make a decision on something which has no answer, to define the unfathomable colour. The colour in real life is ephemeral, I splash about in the tray of the water-colour box and try to get the exact tone, wait for the likeness, but the subject is a moving one. Right at the waterline, where the elements come together, shallow, watery and delicate, they alternately take on each other's appearance, the water becoming sky, the beach becoming water. The brush dashes between the colour pots – mauve, ultramarine, cerulean blue, Naples yellow, crimson and zinc white – and the eye tries to fix the reflections on the water's surface, where all of the pink and dove-grey colours of the sky are present, an endless kaleidoscope, and I am forced to accept a colour tone from my mixtures. It is not a choice of colour but an extract from a process. The state of things is more important. Then the colour flows, is mixed, takes hold of the gull's dark sandy-coloured belly, cuts in, radiates back, dissolves, like reflections from the rings on the water around the gull's leg. The slender moorings to solid matter, which at any time can be broken. What is reality, what is impression. To see into everything and nothing and to formulate something is as if to descend, to make oneself weightless and physically to be part of the whole and be guided by the soul alone, to let oneself DISSOLVE.

This is a highly personal text, marked by a profound personal presence. It describes the concentration when faced with a transient subject, the pursuit of a changing play of light in air, water, feathers … where everything is part of a virtually indissoluble whole – the futile pursuit of the the unremittingly 'moving subject'. The text is in itself a figurative piece, a 'poem', with a subject that seems as changeable as the light. What is distinctive is that the word 'I' occurs only three times in it, twice in the first few lines and once in the middle of the passage. Equally distinctive is that this word 'I' is combined with 'am forced' in two of those three cases (in the third case, with 'splash'). It seems as if 'I' becomes perceptible, even 'real', only in combination with coercion, when the artist is forced to make the impossible decisions, those which in a certain sense clash with the uninterrupted progress of light, reflections, changing colour. The artist ('I') is forced to arrest this process, even to distort it, to have any chance of capturing something of it on the water-colour paper. There-after painting itself takes over the account, on its own, no longer impeded by the artist's 'I'. Painting in itself becomes a kind of fusion with the moment, the transformation – the descent, the weightlessness, the dissolving. And this is an essential piece of information in Lars Jonsson's art: that nature can never be fixed (not even the House Sparrows outside the window), that it is ultimately impossible to determine what is what, whether air, water, land, light or feather. And perhaps not even just impossible, but absurd. The existential question in these pictures is: who is it that descends, that weightlessly forms an integral part of the whole – who is dissolved?

How one chooses to answer such questions is down to the individual's personal view. But as much as this experience can be like ancient magic, perhaps even the same as that felt by the Paleolithic painter at his cave wall, it is just as much connected with something as modern as the telescope, the link which in Lars Jonsson's art has surpassed both the bullet and the camera lens when it comes to giving meaning to the animal in its landscape, and the human being who is watching that animal.

The field guides represent the starting point for Lars Jonsson's artistry in book form. They were followed by three large volumes of drawings, water-colours, oil-paintings and essay-like or lyrical texts (excluding the fourth, with which we are at present occupied): *Ön: Bilder från en sandrevel* [Bird Island: pictures from a shoal of sand] (1983); *En dag i maj* (1990); and *Dagrar* (2000). In a Swedish context these books are most closely affiliated to similar works by Gunnar Brusewitz, in particular the latter's three 'notebooks' from the first half of the 1970s (*Skissbok*, *Sjö* and *Skog*). Lars Jonsson's books, too, have the character of 'notebooks', or sketchbooks, even though they reproduce finished paintings. They are presented in such a way that the reader can sometimes feel that he is leaning over the artist's shoulder and watching him paint straight on to the book: splashes of colour, or simple tests for various shades and hues, are left in the picture margins, or small bits of extraneous material (insects and other things which land on the page of the drawing pad in the open air) are drawn there. This is not, however, a matter of simple illusionism. Rather, the artist wishes to draw attention to the difference which can, after all, be found between the pictures in these books and the scientific ones, those in the field guides.

All three volumes take their themes from southern Gotland, where Lars Jonsson lives. They are portrayals of the same landscape. In addition, they are each distinct 'projects', artistic assignments. At least in the first two, *Ön* and *En dag i maj*, he presents a kind of extract from everyday life in nature, laid bare and given special attention, special scrutinisation. Lars Jonsson has often talked of his interest in the intimacy of close environments, micro-habitats, of which most people are unaware. It is in contact with these that 'perspective is transformed' and the eye changes, becomes open. The book projects in themselves represent such 'extracts', in landscape and time. *Ön* is about a shoal of sand in a shallow sea bay, 'some eighty paces long and at its broadest some thirty paces', which appears and disappears, but which for a limited period constitutes a world of its own, in a unique and perpetually recurring act of creation.

> I did not suddenly awake to the island's riches. It was by chance that I painted several water-colours using themes from the island. But they formed a pattern; they went together. Instinctively I felt close to a secret passage leading to something surprising. There, as I observed in deep concentration and painted, it began. The paintbrush which worked over the paper and the water-colour which flowed out in patterns and shapes formed words. I began to see the opening chapters to a thrilling tale.

He makes it his task to watch and study this world and its colonists, from the moment when the shoal of sand emerged from the shallow sea until the autumn storms annihilate it (only to re-create it another year, in

Sketchbook: Study of American
Woodcock
Morris Island, Massachusetts,
14th September 1995
Water-colour 50x32 cm

28

another place, with a different appearance – the same island, but not the same one). The portrayal of the island is a journey of discovery, in the countryside, not far from his front door. Nothing 'new' happens, true, and he sees nothing that he has not already seen countless times in the same countryside – but by training the telescope on the island itself, and not on the birds that move around in the landscape where the island is situated, he can watch the internal cycle of life with a new eye.

I came to share the essence of the island. It took on almost religious values for me. Its spectacle fascinated, thrilled, enthralled and entranced me. Each daylight hour that I could not share with it filled me with restlessness. In many respects, what happened on the island was a natural biological progression of events paralleled everywhere in nature. A reality existed, and that reality is the seedbed of emotion and fantasy. Perhaps it was the closeness to nature, the feeling of being allowed to take part in something outside the world of man, that had me spellbound. It does not make much difference, for in this situation the island was an endless sea, an inexhaustible ocean of possibilities. One incident succeeded another, and different chords of colour were sounded, only to float away again. Colours, patterns, movements, expressions, sounds and smells constantly gyrated. I entered into the birds' behaviour, understood their moulting patterns, and understood their unrest just before migration. I took part with more and more intensity in these events so that landscapes from far distant places began to paint themselves right inside me and new events took shape when the wind played in a moulted feather.

I knew exactly how the savanna in west-central Africa must appear to the Ruffs; how it cried out and how they were drawn to it; and how the tundra around the mouth of the Yenisei was now beginning to fall silent. I became one with the birds and with the island's world. A force field arose where impulses constantly flowed between us.

This can happen with Lars Jonsson ... the restricted landscape of the island opens almost endlessly out into the world, in an almost 'shamanistic' way. His mention of religion in this context is not really surprising, but what he experiences is founded on a factual, non-metaphorical way of looking at things, observations of 'simple' biological processes.

En dag i maj is also a kind of extract, not from the landscape but from time. Here the 'project' is, as the book's title indicates, to document in illustration and words a single predetermined day, Thursday 18th May 1989, from four o'clock in the morning until '21.59', when it is so dark that he can no longer see what he is writing in his notebook. The day is also a journey in the countryside, which takes him from Riset, Gotland's southernmost headland, to Faludden, just under twenty kilometres to the northeast. The concept of the book is based on a different kind of

insight from that which he investigated in the study of the sand shoal and its life. This one is about the restlessness of migrating birds: they are on passage, the spots where they are observed are temporary stopover sites, and they have to move on ... and their restlessness is examined in detail by Lars Jonsson. His planned route across southernmost Gotland is not unlike that taken by some of the birds, between two flights over open water. He also is travelling, his visits to the different observation points are also marked by haste – he, too, wants to get on, as the 'project' dictates that he does.

But:

On a day like this, when these bushes are filled with migrating passerines, I want to just sit and watch, look for the features of the various species and review them. The birds show themselves only briefly, disappear, and turn up again in the form of new individuals, new faces. Constant surprises, little incidents and minor spectacles, patterns which form and then break up. I never tire of it.

We cannot know it, but perhaps the impulse is just to settle down on the spot and to become self-absorbed, but all the time being forced to leave by a superior will ... exactly what the migrating birds feel.

A tacit assumption in *En dag i maj* is the understanding that the end can never be reached, as nature's richness is always too great, and that this has to be a theme in all wildlife portrayal. Or the knowledge that completeness is never achieved, that a single May day, eighteen hours, is as inexhaustible as the life on a sand shoal – just as it is impossible ever to achieve a definitive picture 'even' of a House Sparrow. Experiencing the moment is an implacable reminder of its transitoriness, how quickly it will vanish, and in Lars Jonsson's intoxicated notes, sketches and texts there is at times an impression of sorrow, but elevated to selflessness, as in this 'June night' from *Dagrar*:

In the setting sun I sometimes feel restless. The colour of the water in the bay gradually merges with the mauve-pink and turquoise-blue colours of the low clouds. Millions of colours and shades touch me. I attempt to capture the slowly diminishing light, paint feverishly, but it goes. It is like a precious article slowly falling to the bottom and there is nothing I can do about it. And yet the gradually fading Nordic twilight is enticing, tantalisingly inviting, so that one is tempted to reach out one's hand towards it. I can still see, draw shapes, mix colours and put brush to canvas. When I look up a final time to check my impression of the colour tone, it has already changed, as if it never existed.

Even the texts in his books are sketches, apparently noted down in the pad with the same hand movement as used for the water-colours. They often start with a quick weather report: air temperature, cloud cover, wind … the atmosphere in which the birds make their appearance, the light in which they reveal themselves, move and rest. He inspects and assesses the immediate vicinity, counts species and individuals, all as a preparation for painting. It is not diary entries that he makes but, rather, 'snapshot notes', brief notes, for the record, or as a kind of training in the unfamiliar world, the birds' world. He may interpose brief thoughts, on the light or on the dominant colours in the landscape and plumages, or toy with observations of the birds' behaviour, and that of man.

Further, the texts are something more than mere commentaries supporting the paintings. They record what the pictures can not show, at least not so clearly: his own feelings for the subject, associations, his thoughts. They may appear factual and lacking in artistic quality, at least in comparison with the water-colours. Closer reading, however, reveals that they are not uncommonly dramatic and unobtrusive accounts of entering the birds' world, or even of identifying with the real life described in them. Here is an example from *Ön*, a passage from 1st or 2nd August.

Warm overcast, muggy, calm. A heavy atmosphere. Not a breath of wind, still, greyness, suspense. We are facing a turning point; and the final breakthrough of autumn. The air feels heavy, the bay is full of birds, the movement only adding to the stillness. A few curlews squeeze themselves through the air. Isolated birds call, but the air quickly closes up again. Greenshank, Grey Plover, a distant Great Black-backed Gull, Lapwing, Swallow, all call their message. Time stands still; for a few minutes, a vacuum is created by the changing weather. One is almost afraid to breathe, knowing full well that at any moment the wind will get up, rain fall, clouds open up, releasing the elements from their bondage. A crucible where everything is enclosed, human beings, animals, plants, rocks, all creation. A plaintive and vibrating call from a young Curlew bursts the bubble, and an east wind cools the cheek and gently begins to stir the blades of grass. I shake my head a little and wonder if really it was the Curlew that set the wind free or if it was the wind that set free a pent-up call.

This is all about a kind of intermediate state and Lars Jonsson calls it 'breathing space' – but there is no element of repose here, no sense of relief. On the contrary, it is a state of strong but intangible exertion, directionless build-up, and strangely deadlocked, restrained, without purpose. A 'non-existence' in which everything is enclosed, the landscape and all that inhabits it at the time – a waiting for departure. The air is muggy, it is oppressive, he notes, and there is a sense of 'oppressiveness' in his words, too, in his perception, a sort of breathlessness. The air is heavy, and despite the bay being full of moving birds there is no real movement; the curlews have to squeeze through the air as if in a kind of inert, resistant, viscous matter. And the words themselves, it seems, come out only reluctantly, in short sentences, odd phrases, incomplete. It is as if the conditions also prevent the language from developing: the words come, but seem all the while about to cease in his broken-off sentences, as 'the air quickly closes up again'. The state prevailing in the natural world is also present in the language, and in the text's restless, almost incoherent comments. Many species call, but with no further effect; everything is waiting in suspense for the state of 'non-existence' to snap, to be broken … which indeed it finally is. Suddenly the call of the young Curlew is heard and the wind is released from the stifling calm, almost in an act of liberation. And only then can the language expand, literally so. The text ends in two long flowing sentences, unbroken by punctuation apart from a single comma in one of them. It is as if the language itself breaks its shackles, shakes off its 'muggy', suspenseful restraint, its irresoluteness, and … really starts to develop.

It is not necessarily the case that this development of the text is designed for literary effect. Perhaps it is more likely to have been intuitive, arising from Lars Jonsson's own presence on that day at that moment in time. 'Non-existence' is, of course, difficult to paint, as it involves a tension within, suspense. He records it in the birds' behaviour: they are in a time phase immediately before departure, but they have not yet launched off on their long flight. This text is thus not just a memo about a change in the weather or a shift between seasons, and it is more than a testimony relating a personal experience of a sultry day and the nervousness of the birds in the bay. It is a representation in words of the birds' moment of departure – the uncertainty, the restlessness and finally the big move, when they are up and away on migration. It is a linguistic representation of the non-human element, the 'ornithomorphic'.

Words can sometimes reveal what pictures cannot, but hardly colour: colours very rarely come through in language. In his writing, Lars Jonsson is often content to use simple ('unmixed') words for colour: yellow, pink, mauve. If more precise details of these are wanted, then we must go to the pictures, where we find all the tints and hues that cannot be expressed in words. Yet in his texts, on the other hand, he may revise a statement on colour, as in this casual remark taken from *Ön*, '9th August':

Sketchbook: Studies of Grey
Partridges
27th October 2001
Pencil and water-colour 50x32 cm

The Grey Partridge is still present in
good numbers in the open cultivated
country of southern Gotland. It is one
of my favourite subjects. Studies were
made of a family party dust-bathing
and resting in a sandy depression on
an open dry meadow. They allowed
me to study them through the
telescope so closely that I was able to
draw minute details around the eye
and bill. The drawings on the left are
of a male, the water-colour on the
right a female.

22.10.01

Sketchbook: Study of Bald Eagle
West Yellowstone,
15th September 1998
Water-colour and pencil 50x32 cm

This bird perched in a poplar on the other side of a narrow and fast-flowing river which ran alongside the road to West Yellowstone, on the border between Idaho and Montana. I parked the car, sat down on an embankment and studied it through the telescope. The clear light and the colours in the background inspired me to take out my water-colours. The afternoon sun shone directly on to it from the front, and the light fell very attractively over the head and the plumage.

W Yellowstone 15·9·98

34

Sketchbook: Studies of Arctic Fox
and Curlew Sandpiper
Zarya, NW Taymyr, 26th June 1994
Pencil and water-colour 50x32 cm

Observations by night during
midsummer 1994. Rolling treeless
tundra. While I am drawing a Curlew
Sandpiper *Calidris ferruginea* which is
proclaiming its territory from a small
mossy hummock, an arctic fox passes
by on the hunt for lemmings.

The sun is a couple of inches above the horizon. The island is in contact with the land. Large platforms of sand lie spread out like delta lands in towards the shore and facing the outer side. A wooden box has been uncovered on the north beach, and on the spit towards the shore nearest to me there is something green-looking, shining somewhat like an emerald. To tell the truth, I have never seen an emerald as far as I know, but before me I see a deep, slightly transparent, obscurely bright green colour. Curaçao is perhaps better, green curaçao shines in the channel on my tropical romantic island.

This is a funny remark. Emerald-green is a colour familiar to many people in Europe, from a school-assembly song about dew-covered mountains, while Ireland is often referred to as 'the Emerald Isle'. We know that emerald is green because that island is famed for its greenness, a beautiful grass-green we might imagine, but doubtless most of us (like Lars Jonsson) have no real idea of the stone itself (dark green, grass-green, the dye substance chromium); emerald-green sounds attractive, quite simply, well known but not very special. This may well have been why he first used the emerald in this passage: the greenness on the island is of the usual sort, the same as everywhere in the countryside, but on the island it is new and a little 'exotic' – it calls for a rather special name, and the emerald in the song immediately comes to mind. Just as quickly it strikes him that this is a cliché and nothing more, so he looks for another word instead and hits on the green liqueur. Curaçao 'sounds' a bit like emerald, exotic, and it corresponds with the appearance of the particular green colour on the sand shoal – curaçao it will be!

But it is not just a matter of colour-matching here. He can use advanced identification tools (Smith's Naturalist's Colour Guide) for that, when dealing on a more serious level. In this case it is more a piece of lighthearted fun; and when he takes the green from the children's song and places it in the sphere of more adult pleasures, it is not the role of Lars Jonsson the painter that he is playing, but that of Lars Jonsson the writer.

This verbal lightheartedness, often coupled with an element of pleasure-seeking, is a feature of Lars Jonsson's portrayal of nature. At any rate, there are plenty of such striking metaphors in his books, and not least in his most recent one, *Dagrar*, where he describes a day in mid-July, and a happy summertime feeling right down to the toes and to the words themselves: 'It is eight o'clock in the evening and the temperature is still 23°, so warm that I want to take off my shoes. The light is coming from all quarters, and the water is warm and yellowish-grey. The Greenshanks call across the sky like berry juice over whipped cream.'

Dagrar is different from the earlier books. It is not an extract, not an overview of a delimited subject. It is the portrayal of a year in four parts, from winter to autumn, and is therefore in a certain sense more traditional than *Ön* and *En dag i maj*. Swedish wildlife art abounds with books on the annual cycle of the seasons (they are a convention within the genre). But in another sense *Dagrar* is not traditional, and from a literary angle the book exhibits a brilliance that sets it apart from the two earlier volumes.

The concept of an 'open frontier' between the human observer and the birds has always been an essential factor in Lars Jonsson's art. In *Dagrar*, the texts have to a great extent become equally valuable interpretations of this concept, the sensitivity which had previously been reserved for the painting. There is a wonderful literary 'impudence' in the writing, when every now and then Lars Jonsson permits himself to exceed the rules of language and semantics in order to describe encounters between man and bird in new and unexpected ways. In the following description of a Curlew, for example, the bird's delightful display literally flows over, in all directions at the same time – the Curlew both pours out its display and drinks it in:

The Curlew gargles, exuberantly pours forth from his golden chalice, indefatigably he savours the drink which ripples from his streaky throat. From his half-closed bill comes a kind of aphrodisiac, a strange perfume of straw, malt, sun and clear springwater. For long he pumps out muffled sounds from his breast, long deep breaths until the liquid breaks forth and runs over, like honey and sun over the cool expectant landscape.

This is just not 'right'; the words do not go together properly. But the impression of the displaying Curlew is shaped by an exuberant thirst for life.

The book's title indicates its subject matter: 'Everything is merely light, reflected daylight, the different lights of the day [*Dagrar*].' The light, and the way it continuously creates forms, matter – air, water, greenery, rock, bird. Lars Jonsson uses his senses in a new way, and his writings possess a remarkable sensitiveness to the manifestations of the landscape – traces of fragrances, micro-climates, imperceptible puffs of wind. The language is open to all that, in a way that reminds us of his predilection for painting white birds, such as gulls, terns, Avocets, small plovers, Magpies; the birds' whiteness is used as a means of portraying light, the nature of the air, temperature. (For white they hardly ever are, no matter how much we try to perceive them as such; the white areas are grey, brown, pink, blue, yellow – or even deep blue, as the male Pied Flycatcher in *En dag i maj*.) This is similar to the way in which the watercolour paintings themselves demonstrate a sensitivity to the play of light, the reflections, the changing lights of the day, where the technical and the existential factors appear to coincide: 'There is no given colour for the evening sky's reflection in the water, yet it still has to be exact, determined by the situation in which I find myself; my own presence is the only true colour.' Lars Jonsson uses the texts in *Dagrar* in order to expand the manifestation of this personal presence, to ascertain its nuances, as in the following circumspect depiction of the invisible landscape, that which is always around us but which can never be fully described. It is a late afternoon in early August:

The air in the yard is warm, stifling, boxed in by tall dark green ash trees and limestone walls. When I leave this spot and wander out into the open, the air feels somewhat cooler and damper, the evening drawing mist from the green pasture. This change in temperature is clearly felt. The moister air gently nips the wings of the nose and bathes the most sensitive fleshy parts of the face, and it feels as if two large cool hands are laid across the shoulders, and pass over the shins. The smell of dry grass comes and goes with the temperature of the air. It is strong, almost pungent, where cool air deposits damp-ness in the hollows of the meadow, it becomes weaker when I approach a bush, and it dies away completely in the mild air under isolated trees along the way. When I reach some big elms, the warm embracing air is there again. I stop awhile, feel for a scent, but it eludes me – perhaps a faint note of lime dust, or of crow feathers. Here the soft sun-warmed air of the day and the dewy air of night play hide-and-seek, like brother and sister. The crows cluster in some whitebeams but scatter when I come wandering randomly in their direction, like soot flakes from an open fire. The juveniles have neat wing outlines, but the adults are moulting and are tatty and ragged.

In *Ön*, *En dag i maj* and *Dagrar*, Lars Jonsson has in various ways taken as his theme something which is short-lived and unique, something which will vanish – the shoal of sand which will be washed away in the autumn storms, the single day in May (which was never 'any one day') and, not least, the changing lights of the day, those microscopically fine processes that take place in landscape and perception, which are never-ending change, movement, an endless progression of variation within a single whole – captured in the moment when the artist becomes part of it.

The metaphor that nature is a 'language' is a common, and perhaps rather careless, one. We have to be able to read, or to translate, the 'book' of nature. This can result in infatuation or in strict science, depending on who is doing the reading. When Lars Jonsson employs the metaphor, however, he makes it more complicated: to him nature is a 'language', tactile like braille, but we are unable to read it, or at least to read all of it.

I read a final sentence from the Dunlins' evening migration by feeling the landscape with my fingers, stretching out my arm to touch the shore and the water. The air is far too soft to take the impressions, I cannot make out the details, and the Dunlins disappear southwards taking their words with them.

There is a sense of frustration in this, of course, but also a paradoxical joy in the knowledge that nature does not have to be put into words,

'understood', for it to have meaning for us. He sees some Swallows land on the shore, take off, 'dance above the sandflies' broad atlas', this going on for a minute or so, and then they are off – and: 'I had something to relate which I think is important, but I never managed really to see what – oh yes, I saw, I saw but … only I and no-one else. Nobody else will ever see what I have seen.'

At any rate, that is where his eye has taken him, to experiences which he cannot put into words, cannot share with others. To a solitude which at the same time is a sharing, which opens outwards to creation and inwards, to the inner landscape of the mind, the senses. Lars Jonsson has described what he sees with scientific objectivity, or in his art with a reverence that can at times be like a secular religiosity of sorts. Maybe it can be said that his knowledge of birds (and their worlds, which are also his and ours) is too great to be housed 'only' in science or 'only' in art, and that he has therefore in a certain sense done away with the boundary between what we call the one and what we call the other. If that is so, then this is most elegant, something for which to be thankful.

By naming the blackness it becomes darker, assumes a tendency, acquires depth rather than background. Darkness is gradually given a structure, a shape and a life in the same way as the light. Perhaps it is the same with the blackness associated with great sorrow or grief, a blackness that seems to have no identity or colour until the soul becomes accustomed to it. It can contain a wealth of shades as great as does pleasure if one is capable of looking into it.

Lars Jonsson has developed his art, his bird studies, into exercises in insight – into the birds' life, and into those nooks and crannies of our own perception of which we are not always consciously aware. He depicts this insight as encounters: not only does he watch the birds, but they watch him back. In many of his pictures the bird, or one of the birds, is turned directly towards the painter (and the observer), looking straight out of the picture, showing no timidity, no readiness to take flight – just an eye meeting our own. What such a look expresses – whether it is inquisitiveness, interest, 'mutual understanding' or what-ever – we cannot be sure. In the opening lines of this book, I wrote that the Hooded Crow in the first volume of *Fåglar i naturen* is looking back and defying us. This is, of course, an interpretation. What the gulls and

Sketchbook: Saxifrageous ground
Wrangel Island, 24th July 1994
Water-colour 50x32 cm

Claytonia arctica
Painted during a visit to this
high-arctic island during the
Swedish–Russian Tundra Ecology
expedition in summer 1994. While
waiting for a Knot to approach more
closely, I lay on my stomach on a bare
hillside and became fascinated by the
saxifrages in the stony ground.

40

the terns 'say' when they meet our eyes in his pictures we do not know, but in the moment of intense mutual presence we can perhaps sense a statement of some kind, untranslatable though it may be.

In *En dag i maj*, he describes such an encounter, with a female Bluethroat:

> I sit down on the ground behind a wall, with lilac bushes and a maple in front of me. The lilac forms an almost mangrove-like jungle at ground level, the sun filtering between the numerous inch-thick branches. Two Lesser Whitethroats, a male Blackcap, a Thrush Nightingale and a female Bluethroat are moving around inside it. The warblers occasionally come and perch in the last rays of the sun and ruffle their feathers as if about to roost: will they stay or are they just resting before nocturnal migration? On one occasion the Bluethroat hops towards me and perches no more than two metres away. With its big black eyes and its expressive face it is just like a bandstand conductor, with erect stance on long legs, and it turns straight towards me. When it bows to take an insect the spell is broken. For a brief while I felt some kind of contact, but obviously it was just food it was after; only with great imagination could one read something else into those dark eyes.

Obviously?

Lars Jonsson is an artist and an ornithologist in one and the same guise. All his ornithological knowledge makes him objective, unsentimental, like a true professional, and it is a critical faculty. At the same time, as an artist, he is supported by what he calls feel, imagination, empathy (entering into the birds' lives) – not as the antithesis of knowledge, but rather as an extension of it. This 'contact' with birds, a theme to which he repeatedly returns in his pictures of them: is it 'obviously' a case of self-delusion?

The question must remain unanswered here.

Only one thing is in fact obvious, and that is that we do not know for certain.

This wondrous uncertainty is what Lars Jonsson paints. When we see his paintings, it becomes, at best, our own.

STAFFAN SÖDERBLOM

Sketchbook: Studies of female Eiders
on wet rocks
Rivet, 6th May 2001
Water-colour 50x32 cm

Rivet is the southwesternmost tip of
Gotland. I spend much time there in
spring and autumn painting sea, rocks
and seabirds. A note at the bottom
left-hand corner states: 7° + N wind
ca 10 m/sec.

42

6.5. Ross. 7° Nordlig vil ca 10 kb/m

Sketchbook: Studies of
White-tailed Eagle
Hamra, 4th November 2001
Water-colour 50x32 cm

In winter, one or more White-tailed
Eagles nearly always perch in a large
poplar at Stuckvike, the small reed-
fringed lake situated near the shore
not far from my studio. I often draw
them when they are looking out over
the lake and the surrounding
meadows. It is windy and their bushy
nape feathers are lifted by the strong
wind; sometimes an odd feather on
the shoulder or breast is caught by the
wind.

44

Sketchbook: Studies of two warblers
Salechard, 18th June 1996
Pencil drawing 50x32 cm

Willow Warbler on left side and
Arctic Warbler on right. Observed in
western Siberia, in tundra sparsely
vegetated with larches, just outside
the village of Salechard on the lower
Ob.

Various birds, probably 1958
Oil-pastel 57x38 cm

You were born in Stockholm in 1952. What are your earliest memories of animals and of drawing? Can you remember when you first became interested in depicting birds and other animals on paper?

I do not have a clear perception of why birds were more interesting to me than anything else. The first drawings I know of in which I made a conscious effort to replicate birds were done when I was four-and-a-half years old. I drew five or six birds on both sides of a piece of paper, a written annotation by my mother dating it to March 1957. They resemble a child's early drawing of humans, and show two pairs of feet on each 'leg' and tails similar to those of beavers. But they were drawn in side-on view, with eyes, a bill and a pattern on the body.

On another drawing which I did when I was about five, a flying Great Crested Grebe is drawn with the breast of a Great Tit, presumably because of a lack of references or simply to liven up its character a bit. The wader in the foreground has blue eggs and a straight bill, but resembles a Whimbrel or Curlew in plumage pattern. I was fascinated by birds' nests and eggs from an early age.

These drawings were made with pastels, a material which I frequently used during my childhood. There is something about these crayons' rich colours and consistency that even today gives me a feeling of exuberance. It fills me with delight to open a new box, remove the cellophane sheet that protects the tips and see the different colours next to each other.

I have another very clear and strong memory of colours from Kindergarten in 1958. We had to weave a small rug in materials of different colours on a miniature loom. I felt a distinct pleasure in the way certain colours belonged together, and I vividly remember how I was mesmerised by the prettiness of pink against a greyish-green and a moss-green hue.

I wanted to be 'the boy with the magic pen', inspired by a children's film which made a lasting impression on me. It was about a boy who had a magical pen. Whatever he drew, the image became a reality. My aim was to make birds come alive by using pen and colours.

The desire to make birds come alive and the experience of nature are two recurring elements in your life since a very early age. You made some drawings in 1959 which your parents saved. The birds in these pictures were even then carefully drawn with the specific characters of each species clearly visible: a Green Woodpecker, a Peregrine Falcon or a Nuthatch. The Green Woodpecker has a barred tail, the Nuthatch a rusty vent etc. Were you already an active birdwatcher at that time?

I was birdwatching a lot, often with my brother Anders, who is one year older. We returned home from our forays in the neighbourhood with frogs, bird chicks, lizards and various caterpillars, and our home was a veritable mini zoo.

The Stockholm suburb where we lived was still immediately adjacent to the countryside. There were cultivated fields, ditches with frogs, and copses where a typical central Swedish avifauna resided. One day, when I was about seven, I came home to get my mother to show her a Green Woodpecker excavating a hole in a large aspen. I had spent the whole morning lying quietly beneath the tree and intensively watching how it frantically chiselled out the hole, wood chips flying everywhere. When I came home, my hair was full of chips.

I also remember how my brother and I often spent evenings huddled on a recess at a skylight window, where we looked out over a steep mountainside and a pine forest which towered aloft behind the adjacent terrace house. He told with great feeling of how he was friends with the birds of prey and had

Birds
April 1957
Pencil 37x50 cm

Green Woodpecker
28th November 1959
Oil-pastel 37x58 cm

49

At the drawing-board
Farsta, 1959

Lars with his brother and sister at Lake
Ågesta, spring 1960

visited the Goshawk, the Golden Eagle and the Peregrine in their nests. I believed every word he said, and really wanted to join him on his next visit. He told me that they were shy and would only reluctantly allow anybody into their circle, but he would ask them. I was maybe five or six at the time.

Children's images and fantasies are often strongly influenced by books. Which books do you remember as important in your development during your earliest school years?

One book I remember was *En gyllene bok om naturen* [The Golden Book of Nature], the tattered covers of which bear testament to my intensive reading of it. Not least, it gave an insight into the mysterious and fantastic world of animal life with its accounts of elephants, anteaters, mammoths and sabre-toothed tigers.

A series of books on animals, published by the Swedish publisher Wahlström for the juvenile market, became very important for me. One example was *Tarka the Otter*, by Henry Williamson. In these books, adventures and experiences were presented from the animal's viewpoint. Another title in the series was *Den ensamma örnen* [The lonely eagle], which my mother read to me when I was about six. In a family of White-tailed Eagles, the female had died and the male had to provide for the two young all on his own; unlike the female, he was not good at cutting up the prey, so the young died. This traumatic tale inspired me to paint a long story, on a 9-m-long roll of paper, about an eagle hunting and feeding his young. The ending of my story, however, was a happy one.

Gotland, the large island in the southern Baltic Sea, came into your life early on, as your family spent its first summer there in 1957, when you were almost five. The nature and abundant bird life of Gotland must have captured your attention from the start?

Yes, my childhood summers on Gotland certainly came to be of great importance in my continuing interest in birds. We rented a small cottage, next to a farm, on the coast. My sister, Eva, was born in 1956 and we then became a family of five. In the summer of 1962, we moved to a small fishing village beside a bird-filled bay, and over the following years I came to spend much of my time there. In this area I became well acquainted with Avocets, small plovers and Shelducks. I learned the plumage characters and calls of migrating waders, and how the species composition and age composition of wader flocks gradually changed over the calendar-year.

My second big interest, after birds, was butterflies. Their patterns and refined colour scales were throughout the 1960s something that amazed me, and they still do. Perhaps there is a connection between my passion for birds and my fascination with butterflies. Both have a lightness of weight and are able to defy the laws of nature, and birds also in a sense pass through a metamorphosis, from egg to full-grown flying creature.

As a boy, I was large for my age and felt that I was ungainly, while perhaps these more ethereal creatures presented the opposite impression. Many people were surprised to see my large figure and rather sweeping movements after first having first got to know me through my depictions of delicate butterflies and birds.

For most children, and in fact also adults, a bird is a bird. Species and the differences between individuals are not seen as anything worthy of particular attention. Can you remember when you actually started looking at variations and trying to compare different birds, to see them as individuals?

At home in Stockholm we had a mounted Goshawk, a dark slaty-grey male with a broad white superciliary stripe and a bright yellow-painted cere on the bill. Our hosts on Gotland, where we stayed from 1957 to 1961, had a large mounted female Goshawk on the wall of their living room. It was greyish with a less distinct supercilium, and had an older-looking appearance. The cere was only lightly painted and had a diluted sulphur-yellow tone. I remember studying this bird with great interest while the others were engaged in conversation around the coffee table. I compared our contrastingly coloured male, grasping an arched reddish-brown pine branch with his wings extended, with this female in soft shades of grey perched on a deciduous branch clad with sulphur-coloured lichens that perfectly matched the colour of her cere. Two birds of the same species, each with its own fragment of nature around it, which in their entirety gave two completely different impressions.

From where does your attraction to artistic expression, which evolved in your early years, stem? Were your parents interested in art?

Both of my parents were interested in aesthetics, but there were not, to my knowledge, any artists in our family. Art was, however, always present in one form or another in our home. My father, Sven Jonsson, started as an apprentice in a butchery and eventually became chief butcher at a grocer's shop. During my adolescence he had a small business, developing and selling interior fittings for shops. He also showed musical talent and was very good at dancing; in his youth he became Stockholm Champion in modern dance at Nalen, the largest dancehall in Stockholm at the time. My grandfather, Edor Jonsson, was a goldsmith. My mother, May, had done some painting in her younger years, and her oils were still present in our cellar. When we children had finished school, she moved to the house on Gotland in 1971, followed later by my father. On Gotland, she worked with textiles and set up and ran a shop for locally made handicraft. The shop was expanded with an art gallery, where I had regular exhibitions. My brother and his family now run the homestead.

At a much later age I realised how important it was that there was a genuine love of art

in our home, that artistic work was respected. Another important aspect for which I am now indebted to my parents is they allowed my talent to develop freely: I was supported by them but was not pushed as a 'child prodigy'. In a drawing competition arranged by the school when I was in the third grade, my drawings were refused on the grounds that 'traced or copied work is not acceptable'. My teacher was quite upset, but my father did not want to make a fuss, as time would tell soon enough.

I know that at that age you were greatly fascinated by birds' nests and eggs. You have talked about how, as a youngster, you tried to build birds' nests and that you also collected eggs. In the first of your five-volume series of guides, Birds of Wood, Park and Garden, *there is a painting of two Icterine Warblers by their nest. Am I right in assuming that this painting is in tribute to the intricate nest structure of these birds?*

I collected birds' eggs for a few years in the 1960s, something over which I have later been remorseful. I was very interested in nests and eggs from my early days, mostly because of their beauty; they had a strong appeal for me. Beautiful eggs, different eggs and the collecting itself attracted me. I read the authoritative *Våra Fåglar* [Our Birds], in the fourth part of which Rudolf Söderberg, in the chapter 'The eggs and nests of our birds', seduced me with these words on the Reed Bunting's eggs:

Eggs 5-6 (4-7), smaller than those of other buntings, ground colour paler or darker greyish (greyish-blue or brownish-grey), beautifully adorned with scattered, partly concentrated at the thick end, round spots and ornate scrolls and thick twisting streaks of blackish and greyish-blue, and often with 'fire-spots' (bordered with red, see Chaffinch); sometimes reminiscent of eggs of Waxwing. Average weight 12.5 cgr. Length 18.22 mm, thickness 13.5-16 mm.

The construction of nests fascinated me just as much as did the eggs themselves. I used to gather moss, lichen, dry grass, cobwebs and any other nest material I could find and, using tweezers, try to put them all together to assemble my own, fabricated nests.

Egg-collecting is, of course, reprehensible, and I was subconsciously aware of this even then, always endeavouring to take only infertile eggs. But at times I would take a fresh egg for the collection, although this never contained eggs from any real rarities.

The lonely eagle, 1959
Oil-pastel 900x40 cm

Grey Partridge, 1966   Ballpoint pen 30x37 cm

Tree silhouette, 1968   Indian ink 39x32 cm

Part of the magic was in finding the nests, to figure out how the bird had chosen its nesting place, to understand its strategy. I do not know how many nests I have searched for and finally found, perhaps hundreds. After many hours of watching a Sedge Warbler, to be able finally to part some meadowsweet stems and find the simple but skilfully built nest with its very small, pepper-coloured eggs would give me an immense feeling of satisfaction.

My favourite was the Icterine Warbler, whose nest was for me the greatest marvel of them all. It was made of dry grass and moss, artistically lined with fine, specially rounded straws and animal hairs. The rim was adorned with thin strips of birch-bark and odd bits of lichen, attached with cobweb. Resting in the deep cup were 5-7 eggs of a beautiful pink, with blackish-red flecks and fine spots. When

the eggs were freshly laid, they had almost transparent shells and they felt incredibly frail.

How did your attempts at artistic expression in your teens come out? Were you inspired by anybody, and was there an artist or a knowledgeable person around you who could give you advice and tips?

The eldest son of our summer neighbour in 1962-68 was some seven years older than me and was very adept at drawing. He drew racing cars with a felt pen, a Rapidograph with interchangeable tips. Technically, it all looked very professional; the black Indian ink was razor-sharp against the glossy sheets of the sketchpad. I remember how I longed for his materials. His subject matter was somewhat foreign to me, but the method of conjuring up light and matter was highly inspiring to me.

Eventually, the technically perfect felt pens became mine, too, and were with me for a long time, at least into the 1970s. Apart from being well suited for drawing birds, they were also perfect for drawing complex patterns of branches. I devoted much time to drawing trees with bare branches, silhouetted against hazy early-spring skies. The graphic patterns of trees and winter annuals in a way became my domains, and I still like to study them.

I often went to the Natural History Museum, and it was there, in 1966, that I saw an exhibition by Staffan Ullström. The major part of the exhibition was of bird drawings made with a black ballpoint pen, with mounted specimens used as models. His technique was extremely clever, and the result had a sense of illusionism to it. His exhibition was a major experience. The images had a sharpness of

Stockholm, February 1968
Foto Rune Bollvik

detail and a lustre that thrilled me. I remember thinking that I had to be able to draw pictures as good as his. Over the follow-ing years, many birds and butterflies were drawn with a ball-point pen, from photographs in books. My mother has told me that they were always scolding me for the lack of ball-point pens in the house – I used up all of them.

I was 14 years old, and thus at an inquiring age and open to influences. I was casting about in various methods of expression, searching for something. An awareness now grew in me that different styles, different techniques and material existed.

In your teens you also join Fältbiologerna, the youth branch of the Swedish Society for the Protection of Nature. Was it at about the same time that you started keeping detailed notebooks, nature diaries of a kind, of your observations and experiences?

Something happens in 1966, and even more so in 1967, when I seem suddenly to become aware of time and my own observations. It is typical that, at around 14 years of age, you start seeing yourself as an individual, looking at yourself from the outside, and start contem-plating who you are and who you want to be. I then began writing my diaries, or reports on outings, with observations of birds and nature, weather, and atmosphere and moods.

ÅGESTA, SUNDAY 31ST MARCH 1968

A couple of shakes of a hand wakes one up and, peering sleepily through fingers, one sees brother standing by the bedside. He looks puzzled and asks 'Weren't you supposed to get up and go owl-watching?' A glance at the alarm clock shows that one has overslept. Ten minutes later, on the bike and cycling unsteadily down the gravel track. Still sleepy, hand dragged through the hair and swearing at the alarm clock. Soon calm down and start to be more interested in the surroundings than in the alarm clock. It is 3 o'clock, or may-be half past. It is pitch dark, not even in the east is there a trace of light in the dark blackish-blue night skies. Over Stockholm there is a neon glow, but that is the only light in the sky. There is not much that compares with cycling in the night, not so much at this time of the year as in early summer, perhaps. I continue along on the frost-damaged country road, and when I pass the last lamp-post only the dark-ness seems to remain. All is silent, and as, after a final push on the pedal, the bike rolls quietly to the abandoned cottage, everything seems perfectly wonderful. I lean the bike against a gable and stretch my legs. It is quite cold, but no wind, which is very important for a success-ful excursion. A faint bluish-violet colour quickly begins to expand in the eastern sky. The sun will probably not be visible over the trees for a couple of hours yet. This period, between the first, barely visible hint of light appearing in the east and the reddish glow of sunlight flooding the woods and meadows, is the most pleasant time of the day. I trot off over the stubble field while the male Tawny Owl calls across the lake. The rapidly chang-ing eastern sky begins to mould the black mass into a silhouetted landscape. The Black-headed Gulls are starting to wake up on the lake, but still only occasional calls are heard from various parts of it. Coots are nocturnal, and their hard 'kowk' calls are audible from all parts of the reeds. At this time of the year the Coot is busy marking out its territory. A Reed Bunting, recently arrived back on its home ground, reels off a rusty song. But I walk quickly on, towards the humming sound of a Lapwings' wings. Her wailing call over the flooded April meadows can be heard in the middle of the night. Down in the marsh, a couple of Common Snipes' rather crake-like

'chicke-checke, chicke-checke, chicke, checke' calls are heard. The sky becomes ever lighter and the sounds ever more plentiful. From inside the wood come the Blackbird's fluting notes and the Robin's crisp and delicate song. The gull lake is coming to life. Wigeons and Teals come whistling past, and the Teals, which like smaller waters, come down on to the meltwater pools. The Mallards and Coots have just left their night roosts in the marsh. A sight which has always fascinated me is the Coot's flight, and tonight I saw one coming flying towards me against a yellowish-red dawn sky with its ungainly legs dangling at a 45-degree angle to the body. The early morn-ing turned to day, and it was not long before the first Skylark rose up over the fields on flut-tering wings, its vibrating song acting more or less like a bell. The bird life was soon in full swing, and the roebuck deep in the forest stopped its barking. In front of my feet Meadow Pipits flew up from last year's dead, dew-laden grass. The Osprey pair had returned from Africa and soared on the winds over the lake, occasionally hovering in one spot over the meadows and marshes. The thrushes were active, and the Fieldfares often glided out over the meadow while giving excited harsh chat-ters. They sound something like a Blackbird whose voice has just started to break. A couple of Mistle Thrushes also flew over. At Balingsta, just beyond the willow bog, a Great Grey Shrike was perched on a telephone wire and was perhaps contem-plating flying north-

Studies of Coot, 1968   Indian ink   20x25 cm

There I was, sitting in front of an exhibit of Ruffs displaying on a bog, trying to paint them. One of the curators happened to walk past, became interested in what I was doing, and returned with the Director of the museum. They asked me to come back a bit later and show some more paintings. Together with my father, I returned a week or so later, when the Swedish artist Gunnar Brusewitz was also present and looked at my paintings – a big moment in my life. I was asked if I wished to exhibit my work in the museum in the following year.

The exhibition at the Natural History Museum was in many ways a starting point for you: you were noticed and the newspapers wrote about you. You do a drawing for the daily newspaper, Expressen, *of the birds at Strömmen, the waterway flowing through Stockholm which in winter holds numerous ducks, swans and Coots, and it is published simultaneously with your exhibition. You are asked in a feature article what your future plans are after school. The National Academy of Arts? And you reply 'No, I don't think so. Some profession where you can be outdoors a lot. A zoologist, perhaps. Or a dentist, so that you can afford to spend a lot of time away in your spare time'. Was dentistry the profession you wanted?*

wards at the midday thaw; it uttered its 'priii' now and then. When trudging around in the marsh at Balingsta, which was now quite deep, I continually flushed Common Snipes, which flew up from my feet with explosive 'keetch' calls. Mewing Common Buzzards in courtship flight and high metallic 'chik' calls of woodpeckers were commonplace as I walked back in happy mood to my bicycle, studying all the new signs of spring that filled the countryland today.

Being a member of Fältbiologerna became important. I entered into a new culture where rare birds, the number of species one had personally recorded, migration counts, and various trips to Öland and the Swedish fjells were topics for discussions, rather more so

than walks in the wood and the nesting material of the Jay. I learned quickly. I started to do illustrations for our local branch's newsletter, and I began to acquire a role as an illustrator.

In 1967, as a mere fifteen-year-old, you exhibit your art at the Natural History Museum in Stockholm. How did that come about?

In the early spring of 1967, the school arranged a week of practical vocational guidance for all students. I had chosen a direction myself, and ended up in a greenhouse where I had to pick out weeds amid a nauseating odour of sulphur. I asked my parents if they could write me a sick-note and instead drive me to the Natural History Museum so that I could paint birds.

At the time, there were a couple of prominent ornithologists in Sweden who were dentists. My father had told me that, if you had your own dental practice, you could earn enough money to close during May when you wanted to be out in the countryside. Furthermore, I had a certain fear of dentists, having just undergone complicated jaw surgery, and perhaps my idea was to keep it closed all the time!

The journalist interviewing me, Lars Holmberg, was a foreign correspondent and very interested in birds. He came to be something of a mentor for me for two or three years. We exchanged letters, and he gave me advice on places around the globe where his work had taken him, tips about remote birding places. To a direct question as to which places in the

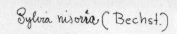

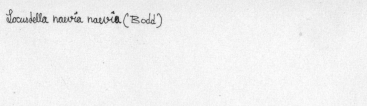
Locustella naevia naevia (Bodd)

Sylvia nisoria (Bechst.)

Lars Jonsson juli/68.

Grasshopper Warbler *Locustella naevia*
and Barred Warbler *Sylvia nisoria*,
July 1968
Water-colour 23x30 cm

55

world he would recommend that I travel for birdwatching, he replied: Afghanistan and the Faroes. I started planning for a trip to the Faroes in summer 1969.

FROM THE DIARY, MYKINES 5th JUNE 1969
The wind has turned to easterly and the sky is unusually clear. The sun beams over the Puffin lands and the luxuriant grass is shining green. Nice weather in the Faroes is a treat you are not spoilt by. The damp mist usually sweeps over the steep, grass-covered cliffs, and the wind is rarely as light as it is today. The Puffins have been lured out of their dark burrows by the sun and the cloudless sky. It is the sun that has caused this mass gathering of Puffins. Not many Puffins are seen to be about when the skies are grey. Puffin country is then empty and deserted, and only their burrows bear witness to their existence. But when the sun appears, hundreds and hundreds of these small auks crowd the ground and the skies. The sheer masses are really surprising when one knows how empty the place can appear to be. Like mushrooms growing out of the ground, they come out of their burrows. Like small gnomes from nowhere, suddenly, they are just there. The heavens are full of fluttering birds. They fly around in circles in enormous flocks, wings whizzing as they pass overhead. At longer distance these flocks look like mosquitoes, comparable in size to the locust swarms of Africa. This year, however, the numbers of Puffins have been heavily reduced. The long winter and the freezing weather reduced the breeding population on the island to a third. And it is almost frightening to see these masses and at the same time to hear the Mykines lighthouse-keeper on Hólmur sigh 'There are no sea parrots this year, the cold took them'. The Gannet and the

Studies of Puffin *Fratercula arctica*, 1969
Pencil and water-colour 27x34 cm

Fulmar are doing better, however, and are present in normal numbers.

To sit in the middle of Puffin country on a sunny day like this is an experience. Studying Puffins with the Atdrop.lantic Ocean and distant, blue mountains as a back Sitting on a rock and watching as they come closer and closer until they finally almost forget their fear altogether. When I walk over the mounds, the place is alive with Puffins flushing in all directions. If one flies, all will fly, and they are seemingly quite frightened, but calmly sitting down usually, as mentioned, gives good opportunities for closer study. With a slight thud they land all around me. Turning the head one way and the other, they look at me in stately manner. A true auk with the characteristic raised back. They look distinctly foppish in their black-and-white tail-coat and colourful bill. The triangular eyes view me slyly, wondering what kind of creature I am. The bold one which is the first to risk jumping on to the rock next to

me is a bit wary. Stretches its wings and looks in astonishment. He is soon joined by some pals which perch on the same rock. Initially they are just as wary, but once they have had a

Mykines, Faroe Islands, in June 1969

56

Studies of Fulmars, Mykines, June 1969
Indian ink 27x35 cm

57

look for while they lie down. A slightly bolder Puffin takes a few more steps and settles. It is quickly followed by a couple more, and so on. Soon they are not far from my rock. The small, plump-bodied birds lie listlessly, peering in the sunshine. The Puffin is not very vocal, but there is still noise around. In the skies above, some Kittiwakes are constantly squabbling over a piece of nest material, maybe some Arctic Terns give an alarm call over a passing skua. In the background the Gannet can always be heard croaking and the Fulmars cackling from up on the cliff.

Your diary entries at this time bear testament to the fact that it is nature, the birds, that attract you most and that you feel a certain sense of loneliness, and a stroke of youthful pessimism over the role of mankind casts a shadow over your notes. Even as a child, you were already attracted – as we have seen – by being part of nature, the boy sitting up in the tree. This is not only a strong tradition in Swedish literature, but also has roots in British romantic literature or the American dream about 'Forest life at Walden', where nature purges man of the shabby untidiness of civilisation and human life. Were you a romantic young man who turned your back against human life and took Nature as a refuge and conversation partner?

I felt a strong romantic longing for nature as if for a friend. I felt at home out in the countryside, where my imagination and my feelings were unleashed. I have myself the impression that my diaries from that time reflect a certain sense of being an outsider, and that is in fact how I felt. I was tremendously focused on nature, and I often felt that I was alone, standing outside, watching.

It was art that eventually released me from the feeling of being an outsider. I had an exhibition at school in spring 1970 and through this came into contact with Pär, a boy of the same age who also painted. We became friends, and we socialised during the last year of secondary school and during the 1970s. Together with my brother and his friend, we planned to travel to Africa after we left school – to migrate south like the birds.

Mykines, 1969
Indian ink 33x42 cm

Bedstraw hawkmoth
Hyles gallii, 1970
Water-colour and gouache 17x18 cm

58

'ON SPRING': FROM THE DIARY 1968
As if by a stroke of magic, the aspen stems and the pine forest darken. Dripping with wet, the trees stand out in the winter landscape on the south slope. The sun, just risen, instils life in the still, heavy snow. For three months the snow has covered ground and roofs like a heavy mattress, but now, inspired by the warm winds and the warm sun, it is everywhere astir. The normally sluggish snow has begun to liven up and there is water running and dripping everywhere. I think that I appreciate the snow most when it melts, on the first warm spring day. Facing the south wall and feeling the sunrays tickle the face, and at the same time listening to the endless splashing and dripping. The first days of the thaw are special, there is something about the air. Maybe it is the smell from the forest that produces this feeling, or just the warmth. I think that it is the combined forces of spring, from the minutest details to the mild wind, that give us that feeling, the feeling of the May lilies of the valley, and glorious summer days in the forest where wild strawberries grow. Mild winds blow through the forest and pull at the twigs and branches. The snow is heavy and wet, you could wring the water out of it.

Soft winds played in dreary black birch twigs, and I felt for a while how I encountered overwhelming forces of spring on the Siberian tundra. You are never as thirsty as when easterly winds cause the solid icicles to drip. If only I could drink up a mountain lake or could breathe in all the air at once. Then, maybe, I could experience the spring as it should be experienced. An immense 'joie de vivre' streams through me and I feel my strength. It is long since man left the cradle of nature, and

Olive tree, Mallorca, January 1970   Indian ink 26x33 cm

he does not feel spring's arrival in the same way as those who live in it. Incapable of capturing all of spring's splendour, I breathe in the wind and watch the play of Jackdaws. Like pieces of charred paper rising from a bonfire, they soar together on the mild spring breeze. Around man's tower blocks and factory chimneys, over green fir tops and majestic pine crowns, they sail. I can hear their ironic laughter over the city's plethora of monuments to mankind's idiocy. They think and ponder on how human beings can have such wrong ideas about the joys of life, trying like fools to make life enjoyable through ideas and inventions. The first thing that existed in this world was nature, and there is nothing more joyous. Imagine if I could experience just a second of their joy in spring, a second or even a tenth of a second. I think of how the Golden Eagle, refreshed by the daytime thaw,

launches out from its cliff. It flies leisurely up along the ridge of the fjell in the obscure light, and when it reaches the top it hangs in one spot for a while, wings flapping. And then, against a red sky and bog pines, it launches itself downwards or, perhaps more correctly, just stretches its wings and sails down along the mountain ridge – no, it's no good describing it, it has to be seen for yourself.

A male Greenfinch sings from a perch among the wet birch twigs, swaying to and fro in the wind sighing through the treetops. The trilling of larks and the Starling flock twisting over a patchily snow-covered field constantly resound in the memory. The time will soon come when one is fooled by the rippling water into believing that the lark can be heard over the meadow. But we have still to wait, yet aware that spring will never let us down.

59

Studies of Black-eared Wheatear
Turkey, May 1978
60   Water-colour 36x48 cm

You finish school in the spring of 1971, and in the autumn of that year you, your brother and two friends travel to Africa in a Volkswagen minibus – an adventurous trip which takes you through Europe, North Africa, through the Algerian part of the Sahara and into Niger, then on through Nigeria to Cameroon. Why Africa? What attracted you to that region?

The adventure, the yearning for freedom. Africa had an appeal, I remember reading in *Birds of East and Central Africa*. Somewhat naively, I fantasised about discovering a species new to science, preparing myself for how to sketch it if it, the unknown bird, suddenly turned up. My dream as a child was to become an explorer, like the Swede Sten Bergman. The trip to Africa was our boyhood dream realised, but not exactly in the way we had imagined. There were many mishaps but, as the years passed, the crises and troubles we went through evolved into the core of the whole experience. We left Sweden in September, driving via Paris and Barcelona to Tangier, then into Morocco, into Algeria and down through the Sahara and into Niger. We travelled through Nigeria to Cameroon, where the car gave out and we almost ran out of money.

We came to a standstill in the middle of the Sahara when a main steering-column bolt broke. My brother hitched a lift with another vehicle to Tamanrasset to try to get a new one. After a couple of days he returned with a 'new' bolt welded together from half of our damaged one and another half from a scrapyard. When we tried to fit it, however, we realised that the cotter needed to attach it to the steering column was missing. It had disappeared somewhere in the sand when we detached the broken bolt. Our lives depended on finding the hairpin-sized cotter. We spent 24 hours systematically taking handful after handful of sand and then sifting through it on a deflated air bed. We found it. But by then the battery was dead, its water having evaporated. But rescue arrived in the shape of a Land Rover carrying ten or so people, who were able to give us a push-start.

We experienced one of the most magical moments in Niger, in the Sahel region, when we pitched camp in a light gallery forest where the rainy season's precipitation had created a shallow lake. We had bought a fresh shoulder of goat or lamb in a village which we tried to prepare over an open fire. It was incredibly leathery, and we finally had to cook it in a pot in our field kitchen – we felt that we really were in Africa. By Christmas we were home. In January 1972 I became ill with malaria and spent some time in hospital.

FROM THE DIARY 26TH OCTOBER 1971
The closer to Tahoa we came, the more villages and livestock there were, villages that fulfilled all expectations and dreams about Africa. Mud huts, bare-breasted women, children and men with bows and quivers, rings and earrings.

We stopped for the night some 30 km before Tahoa. The site was used for grazing livestock, as evidenced by the animals' hoofprints and the trampled grass. Right beside it was a forested area with water, much as yesterday.

The short, intense experience that manifested itself for a brief period before dark struck me for a long time and will always be in my mind. Black Kites were migrating at leisurely pace across the yellow-orange sky, their perfectly measured wingbeats interspersed with glides rendering me speechless. Glossy Starlings with long tails, their calls echoing among the tree trunks, doves whose owl-like calls hummed and rolled from all around. It is impossible to relate the atmosphere, but it is ever present and crystal-clear in my head.

Grilled a shoulder of lamb and had it with couscous in the evening.

When you came back from Africa were you then totally decided on your future choice of profession? Did you never think about reading more, studying zoology or becoming something other than an artist?

To become a painter, to make a living out of art and writing, was a decision that had slowly taken over my thoughts ever since my exhibition at the Natural History Museum. I knew that I wanted to paint, but painting lacked a definite structure. Despite having already had several exhibitions and having sold some work, I felt isolated, left to create a future for myself on my own. I deputised as an art teacher in the winter of 1972. During that time I visited many exhibitions, often at the Thiel Gallery in the Djurgården in Stockholm. It was the museum with most paintings by Liljefors, and with other important Swedish painters from the turn of the century, such as Carl Larsson and Anders Zorn, well represented.

THURSDAY 13TH JANUARY 1972
I finished Albert Engström's biography on Anders Zorn yesterday evening. The final sentence concluded with the words that nobody could fill the empty void which 'Anders' had left behind. His entire history, his life as a person and as an artist, made a strong impression on me, and I had the same feeling as Engström felt over his death when I had finished reading. The book held me in suspense and occupied all my faculties.

Went to Ågesta around 11 o'clock to do a bit of drawing. It was quiet, winter. Noth-ing else but Ågesta and winter. The snow was some 10 centimetres deep, the air not that cold, perhaps 2-3 degrees below zero, and the landscape silent and showing only the wintry blue and milky colours.

Doing a water-colour sketch, which I completed at home, and a study of a wood-pile. A cat, like a Persian long-haired but with dark rustic pattern, provided me with com-pany in the shape of a soft, woolly creature.

In spring 1972, I applied to The Royal Acad-emy of Fine Arts in Stockholm. I submitted a number of drawings of Jonte, our boxer dog, several studies of birds and a couple of water-colours, but I was turned down. It was a disappointment, even though I was told that few people lacking formal training are admit-ted straight away. At that time politically oriented art was very dominant in Sweden – art was supposed to carry a political message, to be part of the socialist class struggle.

I do not in fact have any idea of the reason-ing behind the admissions board's decision, but I can now see that my submitted samples were not very demanding or expressive, and were perhaps even weak in their impact. Maybe this rejection influenced the direction I took, with nature and birds becoming even more prevalent. Most of the time I was outdoors painting water-colours or studying birds in Sweden or on trips abroad.

If one reads your diary from the beginning of the 1970s, it seems that all your attention is directed at nature and the various activities of birds. There seems also to be a strong yearning for colour, for light, but you talk most often about your drawing. Did you think about doing larger oil-paintings, too, during these years? After all, you did want to be admitted to the Royal Academy of Fine Arts and become a painter.

I was very focused on drawing, on getting shape, movement and light by using black-and-white media. During my secondary school years, I wrote in a note in my diary that I was fascinated more by Zorn and the thin water-colours of Carl Larsson than by the heavy paintings of Liljefors, which I now find a bit surprising. The idea of the old academic training was to start with drawing, first one year in the 'school of principles', where one drew geometrical figures and marble statues, copies of the old masters. In the second year you were allowed to start drawing from live models, and not until the third year was colour introduced. I can, in fact, understand the idea behind this, that you must learn to master drawing before colour is allowed in. To express oneself in colour requires a certain degree of maturity, you need to load the colour with a measure of life experience. For several years I had myself drawn birds in pencil and Indian ink, pad after pad of them, almost like a madman.

I wanted to expand and improve my knowledge systematically by drawing in the presence of the subject. I was outdoors with sketchpad and water-colours if not every day, then as often as I could be. In summer I was on Gotland; and in autumn and early spring at Ågesta, a bird lake south of Stockholm. I had started painting in oil seriously during the summer of 1972 and, in retrospect, I think that I was on the track of something here.

ÅGESTA 6TH SEPTEMBER 1972
A perfect day. Summer warmth but without renouncing the clear air of September. The sun shone persistently from morning to evening. The scattered morning clouds were quickly forgotten.

The surface of lake Ågesta was as calm as a mirror between the reedbeds and water lilies. Coots and Moorhens emerged from the reed clumps and foraged among the lily leaves and rotting vegetation. Nutcrackers shuttled over the increasingly reddening reeds. Sometimes towards the hazel slopes to the west, when slim with accomplished wingbeats and short glides; sometimes with overfull crop and then with fluttery and unbalanced flight towards the spruce forests.

A Bluethroat sang by the flat rocks on the east side and was joined by a congener giving 'track' calls. Later, I flushed and heard at least three by the pumping station, where a Common Snipe and some Reed Buntings also took to the air from the increasingly copper-coloured sedge.

The lake had the company of two or more Common Buzzards during the whole time I was sat painting. Sometimes solitarily, sometimes together, they hung weightlessly in the air, spiralling towards the sun.

Some Tufted Ducks, Great Crested Grebes, Pochards and one Goldeneye, together with the Coots, rippled the dark reflection of the oak forest on the lake's sur-face and created the most wonderful of subjects…

Self-portrait
Oil on masonite
46x50 cm

Vinternatt i Farsta
[*Winter night in Farsta*], 1977
Oil 110x70 cm

In 1972, you have your first exhibition jointly with Gunnar Brusewitz, Harald Wiberg (1908–1986) and Allan Andersson (1906–1979). Did it feel as if you were then part of a cultural community of Swedish contemporary wildlife artists?

My bonds with these artists were perhaps strengthened when I was not accepted by the Academy. We took part together in a series of exhibitions over the coming years, and being with these older colleagues was very stimulating. Gunnar Brusewitz, who had himself left the Academy in his youth, spoke in soothing terms – there was nothing for you there! He meant a lot to me, as friend and mentor. When he told me, as early as 1968, that I would be able to make a living from drawing and painting, this instilled expectations in me. He made it possible for me to realise that this could actually be a profession: a youthful dream was turned into something concrete and highly feasible. In my own watercolours from this period I can see the strong influence of Brusewitz. I often think about this today when I see young artists imitating my own way of painting. One has to have a role model at a certain stage of one's development. Brusewitz was such a model for me. To find one's real self as an artist, it is sometimes necessary to paint through others.

Harald Wiberg was my second hero. His awesome eye for the animal and his aptitude in drawing were unique. First, he was an supreme, unrivalled drawer. He was the link in the chain to Bruno Liljefors. For a young artist, it is easy to believe that easy and assuredness with which the foxes and elks flowed from Wiberg's hand were the manifestation of pure genius. But Wiberg told me how, for several years, he had gone almost daily to the zoological garden in Stockholm and made drawings by the elk enclosure. The knowledge of an animal's appearance and pattern of movement, and an insight into whole character, stem from the analytical eye that is a precondition for drawing.

Allan Andersson, together with Wiberg, belonged to the generation after Liljefors. He worked mainly with oil-colours and was heavily influenced by Liljefors's work. Andersson was an emotionalist, both his drawings and his brushstrokes were searching, sometimes a bit cautious. He was, above all, a painter, and a sensitive colour treatment and a strong feeling of presence were borne in his pictures. It was partly through his work, exhibited at the Natural History Museum in 1968, that my eyes were opened to the paintings by Liljefors.

You become established as a bird artist and ornithologist at the beginning of the 1970s. You write and illustrate papers, and publish a series of illustrations in both Swedish and foreign journals. In the autumn of 1973, you are invited to produce a series of field guides on European birds. Did you feel from this moment on that birds were now part of your adult life? One of the papers you write was called 'Characters of waders'. What kind of characters in birds attracted you?

I have had a great interest in field identification from the moment when I first saw *A Field Guide to the Birds of Britain and Europe.* Phenomena in the world of birds, such as the great migration flyways, wildernesses and vast riverine deltas like Las Marismas and the Camargue, appealed to me. The driving force to travel, to visit exotic countries and to develop complies in some way with both the zoologist's and the artist's roles, and I have always felt that I am involved in both.

To study individual birds carefully, and then draw them, is probably what has been closest to my heart since I was about five. I feel comfortable with simply sitting still for long periods and watching birds, perhaps waders more than any other. Getting close to the bird, understanding it in the tiniest detail, is, in a way, my vocation. In 1972 I made many studies of dead birds, a way of trying out the water-colour technique on the

Gunnar Brusewitz, Lars Jonsson
and Harald Wiberg
Kvismaren 1974
Foto: Anders Zetterman

64

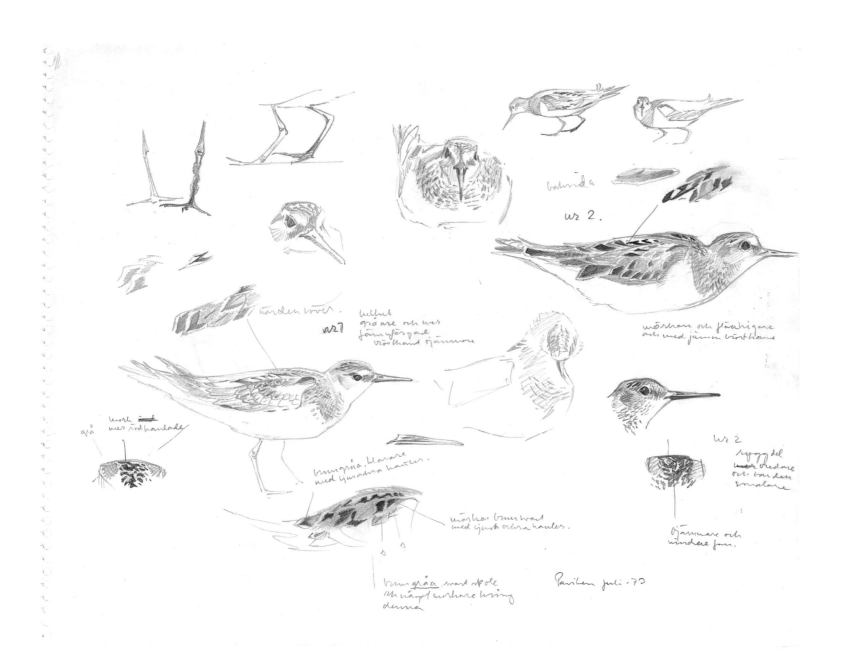

Studies of two Temminck's Stints *Calidris temminckii*
Paaviken, Gotland, July 1973
Pencil 33x42 cm

65

View towards Hoburgen Lighthouse,
29th May 1973
Water-colour 37x56 cm

Wader studies at
Pasvik in Finnmark,
Norway, June 1973
Foto: Mart Marend

66

structure of the feathers and soft parts, their colour tones and the effect of patterns. The summers of 1972 and 1973 were devoted to very close and intense studies of, among others, waders and ducks, going into the minutest detail. I think that I made some discoveries here, I see characters that are not shown in the commonly used identification literature, and this evolves into a kind of pioneering work for my future guides.

In summer 1973 I have an exhibition at Visby, where the paintings I show include several done with gouache colours on tinted paper and based on my detailed studies. In autumn of that year I am invited to produce a bird guide, and most pieces of the jigsaw then fall into place. From this autumn onwards the bird guides dominate my professional life. This gives me the identity which I have in many ways been seeking: I am paid for painting birds, I become a bird-painter-. The bird guides became my own 'academy of arts'. Through this I acquired a work discipline, I practised my water-colour techniques and I travelled a lot in Europe. Often alone, not because I did not want

company, but because on my travels I was in a world completely of my own, engaged in studying and sketching birds. All European species had to be searched for and studied, females, males, in autumn plumage and winter plumage. Calls were to be transcribed, habitats noted, behaviours described. On the whole, I never missed an opportunity to watch birds, and after dusk set in I sat in some hotel room and put together the day's notes, coloured in sketches, and made water-colours while still fresh in my memory.

In your private life, things change during the 1970s. In 1975, you move from your childhood home, the suburban terrace house, to an apartment in central Stockholm, and in autumn that year you buy a large house in the southern part of Gotland, where from spring 1976 onwards you start to spend much of the year.

When I had started working on the bird guides, my confidence in my professional role grew and I also received a monthly advance against future royalties. When I signed the contract on the house in autumn 1975, the

Wood Warbler and apple blossom,
1973
Gouache 31x24 cm

Brooding Eider, 1973
Oil 42x50 cm

Outdoor easel with 'Brooding Eider',
Eider in background. Gotland, 1973

first two volumes were near publication. This was probably the natural explanation for my looking for a place of my own, and southern Gotland was where I wanted to live. In autumn 1974 I was regularly down at the southern tip of the island, Hoburgen, following the autumn migration. I felt very inspired by the landscape of southern Gotland.

My first two books were published in March 1976, and I had an exhibition in April that year. I sold many of the original paintings for the books, and when I took possession of my house in May I was able to pay the first instalment. In the grounds surrounding the house I was greeted by four different Red-footed Falcons, a species as beautiful as it is rare. I took this as a good omen and I felt that I had come home.

The period between 1974 and 1979 is to a great extent devoted to the work on the bird guides and associated trips. Among other countries, you travel to Greece, Spain, Morocco and Turkey to study birds. Do you have time to paint anything else, apart from pictures for the guides? Is there room for your artistic ambitions and ideas during these years?

The work on the books meant that art had to take a back seat. My inquiring efforts when, in the summer of 1972, I painted in oils never matured and were in a way put on hold. But thoughts about art and free painting were still with me, and from time to time I did actually manage to paint more freely. So far as exhibition work is concerned, my participation in 'Animals in Art' in Toronto, Canada, in 1975 is important. I sent a painting of a female Eider brooding, painted in 1973. In the exhibition catalogue I find, for the first time, that there are other wildlife painters in North America besides those, such as Bob Kuhn and Robert Bateman, whom I have come across through field guides.

A large water-colour of Mistle Thrushes, painted in autumn 1974, felt like an artistic turning point. I considered that, in this, I had

not only replicated the birds accurately, but also found a composed colour treatment and an exciting play of light. By painting the dark spots paler and the pale areas more saturated, the contrasts on the shaded parts of the birds were reduced. This created an impression of a layer of air between the birds and myself as observer, the air becoming visible when the sunlight catches particles in the air.

The large house had plenty of room for painting in oils and I did some large-sized pieces of work. I made a portrait of my brother and painted subjects from my garden, such as juvenile Magpies in the lilacs, apple trees and Common Gulls on the lawn at dusk. I also painted some self-portraits. The oil-paintings from the 1970s are inquiring ones, sometimes like water-colours, sometimes more in pointillist style. I can myself feel an ambivalence towards some of these oil-paintings when I look at them now. I did, however, paint several water-colours in which I consider that my own personal presence could be found, one of them being of a dead Raven which I painted in 1977. It addressed the viewer in a pitch that belonged to somebody other than than my idols; perhaps it was my own voice.

The late 1960s and the early 1970s are at the same time a period of student revolts and a surge of left-wing activity. Did you ever feel that you or the art which you were busy working on were part of a bigger, comprehensive picture, or were your activities separated from those which occupied many others of your generation? How did you feel that your art during this period fitted in with that of your contemporaries?

I have always been interested in contemporary art and was a regular visitor at exhibitions in Stockholm during the 1970s. My paintings, however, have never been in tune with that which has been the dominant concern of contemporary art. And, even if I have taken up some elements from

Mistle Thrushes
Hoburgen, 15th October 1974
Water-colour 77x56 cm

contemporary art, my own attitude has developed comparatively independently of the trends in style that have been prevalent at the time.

I felt enormously committed to environmental issues and often reflected over how I could express this through art. No matter how much I turned it over again and again in my mind, however, I could never find an honest way of expressing it artistically. The American authoress Rachel Carson's alarming book on environmental destruction, Silent Spring, had a very strong impact on me when I read it at the end of the 1960s. I had personal experience of mercury-poisoned Pheasants on Gotland and felt great anguish over all the threats facing us. The cover and title pages of Silent Spring were crammed with drawings: sewage pipes, injured and dying birds, factory chimneys etc.

I know that I tried to figure out how to express my position on this situation in my works, but I did not get any farther than that. When I tried, it gave me a feeling of falseness; I have always had difficulty in submitting my pictures to an ideology. Despite my being engaged in many issues, the contemporary political debate had very little to do with 'my' relationship with nature. My way of looking at the world around us had a filter of impressionism rather than one of socialism. In the south Gotland landscape I was spiritually more with van Gogh and Gauguin, or the Scandinavian painters of the turn of the century.

Common Buzzard and Crows, 1978
Water-colour 36x48 cm

Study of dead Raven, 1977
Water-colour 50x70 cm

Warblers, 1983–90
Illustration for *Birds of Europe with
North Africa and the Middle East*
Water-colour and gouache 35x26 cm

Above right:
Willow Warbler *Phylloscopus trochilus*
Centre:
two Wood Warblers *P. sibilatrix*
Below:
Icterine Warbler *Hippolais icterina*,
spring and juvenile in August

The major part of your time in 1974–79 was occupied by Fåglar i Naturen, *the series of five books that established you as an internationally renowned bird artist. These books laid the foundation for the large volume* Birds of Europe with North Africa and the Middle East, *which has been published in eleven languages in Europe. The books contain thousands of bird portraits, many of which give an impression of a personal meeting with the individual bird – have you seen and sketched all of these birds?*

I have always strived to base my illustrations in these books on my own field sketches and observations. I can refer many of these individual birds to a particular sketch or experience. The reason is not just a confidence in my own vision but, equally important, the fact that the very desire to paint emanates from my visual impressions. The optimal situation for me is to paint a specific individual that I have studied and that I know to be typical of the plumage I wish to illustrate. It is more inspiring to tell a story from one's own experience. It is also the case that deviations from or interpretations of personal impressions create life, while the same things easily become mistakes when taken from other people's experiences, models or photographs. The sketch drawn by oneself is therefore the obvious starting point. Thomas Bewick realised this when he embarked on writing his bird books in the 1790s. He writes in his 'memoirs' that when he began his great work he decided not to copy the work of others, but to keep as close to nature as possible.

There are always minor displacements in a bird's appearance in relation to the ideal image, the stereotype. A toe on one foot becomes crooked when set down, the tertials of one wing overlap those of the other, a wing-covert is unmoulted and differs from the rest, the wind ruffles the neck feathers and creates a little shadow, and so on. All these minor variations are often what creates a sense of life. It can be very difficult to contrive these small chance circumstances in the studio. They rarely acquire the same immediacy or life-like feeling as when they are observed and sketched in the field.

A work such as that of illustrating the birds of an entire continent surely demands a knowledge of hundreds of species in different plumages and at different ages. Even though you have travelled widely around Europe to study different species, there must be some birds that you have not sketched. Is it not difficult to make a convincing portrait of a bird that you do not know so well?

When working on the first five volumes, I tried to plan itineraries that would enable me to get to know all of Europe's bird species. Despite this, I still had to depict a few species which I had not really seen at all. A single sketch of a fleeting encounter with a bird makes a big difference, though. I do then at least have an impression to take with me when I later go through and evaluate other reference material to complete the drawing.

Strangely enough, it is the commonest birds that are the most difficult to portray convincingly. Illustrating a juvenile Dunlin or a Willow Warbler can be the greatest challenge. I make greater demands of myself when I know a bird better. It is also the case that most ornithologists have a mental picture of what a Robin or a Blackbird, for example, looks like and they seek confirmation of this picture in the bird guides.

I have put an enormous amount of effort into my Willow Warblers. I know exactly which appearance I am looking for, but as the bird gradually appears on the paper my certainty weakens and I start having doubts. It becomes artificial and unreal – looking like a Willow Warbler but still not one. This is typical for some genera, and the small leaf warblers of the genus *Phylloscopus* belong to this group. When I sketch these birds in the field, I more often feel that I am on the right track – and this is possibly connected with the nature of the sketch, the fact that the less well-defined details are more excusable. A greater variation can be incorporated in a sketch; it is more exact because of its lack of definition.

Newly arrived Redstart, May 1997
Water-colour 32x25 cm

Study of preening Curlew, July 2000
Water-colour 35x48 cm

Awaiting the right wind
Golden Plover
7 May 1996
Water-colour 25x32 cm

How can something be more exact by lacking definition? Is it not the correctly depicted details that create a feeling of truthfulness to nature?

In my field guides I am striving to convey a realistic impression, which is very different from the sum of all details. Each bird has a shape, typical postures and a pattern of movements which in some cases are the key to their appearance, perhaps more so than details of plumage. For most species, however, a combination of general impression and precise depiction of details can be made.

For me, it is important to give the bird a distinct shape, in other words the entirety of the three-dimensional body that a bird represents. Light plays an essential part here.

On a moving bird, the light plays a major role in presenting the shape. In some cases, though, the plumage pattern has evolved so as to break up the shape of the bird when it is crouched on the ground or on the nest. A Curlew is nonetheless always 'more shape than pattern' when standing in the open, while on a brooding Curlew the detailed pattern of the plumage predominates over the shape.

In many original water-colours by early masters such as the Frenchman Jacques Barraband (1767–1809) or John James Audubon (1785–1851), the feathers are beautifully and softly washed with paint. The quills are only partly indicated. When the works were then transferred to copperplate, the feathers became more 'picked out' when the etchers

shaded them by using fine engraving tools with a pointed scraping needle. This continued to a certain extent in the large illustrated collections of engravings of the mid-1800s, despite the fact that the originals were printed using a softer lithographic technique. This stylistic feature survives even today as a way of expressing richness of detail, but in water-colours these 'etched-in' details can to my eyes be more irritating than pleasantly illusory.

I am striving for a balance between details and the bird's essentially reclusive nature – the fortuitous nature of its presence before us. It is just the moment, the experience of the encounter with an individual bird in the wild, that I wish to convey equally as much as factual content.

Small waders of the genus *Calidris*,
1982–83
Water-colour and gouache 35x25 cm

Top: Little Stint *C. minuta* in May, July
and moulting in August
Centre: Red-necked Stint *C. ruficollis* in
July and in early June
Bottom: Western Sandpiper *C. mauri* in
June and in August

Jacques Barraband: Caspian Tern
Copperplate (detail)
From Marie Jules César Lelonge de Savigny,
Système des Oiseaux de l'Egypte et de la Syrie

Skins of Grey-necked Bunting *Emberiza
buchanani* and Cretzschmar's Bunting *E. caesia*
Foto: Krister Mild

Thomas Bewick: Dunlin in winter plumage
From *The History of British Birds, Waterbirds* 1804

76

*In some cases, you must presumably still rely on ref-
erence material other than your own sketches and
impressions in the field. Which facilities and which
sources of information are available and should be
used when painting birds for a field guide?*

To be able to depict all species in a large
number of plumages, one has to rely on many
different sources. The common thing in this
context is to make use of skin collections.
Most natural history museums house scientific collections of prepared birds, which consist
of stuffed specimens lying stretched out in
drawers and lacking the glass eyes of
mounted specimens. These are useful when
comparing larger or smaller series of a certain
bird in a specific plumage. An individual
representative of the species can easily be
picked out from such a series. The skins offer
a means for detailed study of colours,
patterns and structure of the species and of
individual feathers. They do, however, have
their limitations, and patterns and colours
can easily be misinterpreted.

Well-preserved specimens with fresh,
undamaged feathers can often be found in
well-kept collections. In contrast to these,
stuffed or mounted birds often have
somewhat worn or disarranged feathers, and
they show a number of features that are
normally not encountered on a living bird.
Many bird-painters who lack reference to the
living bird often become enchanted by the
minute details on the mounted bird, which
give the painting a feeling of exactness. It is
commonplace to see pictures which
uncritically replicate mounted birds, where
the 'artist' has depicted all the smallest details
meticulously, including the shortcomings of
the taxidermist. The result is a picture of a
stuffed bird. The pattern of larger feather
tracts is often very easy to interpret from
fresh skins, whereas facial patterns, especially
of smaller birds, are often totally or partly
lost during preparation of the skin. If you
look, for example, at Arthur Singer's

gouaches in *The Hamlyn Guide to Birds of
Britain and Europe*, the facial patterns of the
passerines and the birds' postures are the
least convincing. He worked mainly from
skins for this book.

A recently dead bird offers great possibilities for close study. Other bird-painters
and I have a weakness for picking up birds
killed by traffic, something that our fellow
travellers do not always appreciate. This is,
however, forbidden in America. Something of
life is still to be found in a recently dead bird.
Painting from such a bird is a fantastic
opportunity to learn about the qualities of a
bird plumage. It is easy to understand the
sense of proximity that many of the great
19th-century bird-painters achieved through
being able to use recently shot birds – as, for
example, John James Audubon and Louis
Agassiz Fuertes. This had already been
established by Bewick in his day: after having
started to engrave from drawings made from
stuffed birds, he declared that he had not
been working on it for long before he
discovered the big differ-ence between stuffed
animals and animals living in the wild. At
that time, of course, artists did not think of
placing the stuffed animal in the correct
posture or whether the different layers of the
plumage were in the right positions in
relation to each other. Bewick goes on to say
that he had always taken great pains to put a
disarranged plum-age into the proper shape,
but adds that he was never happy with the
result. He was forced to wait for newly shot
birds or live ones.

The photograph is perhaps another resource that can be made use of in this context. The photograph is an exact imprint, a replica of nature. Even so, one can feel that the photographic picture – in the context of a field guide – while certainly producing an exactness, is incapable of lending a genuine presence to the individual bird. It is at one and the same time too exact and too general.

The photograph is undoubtedly a true 'cut-out', but it is not obviously true in relation to our experience, our interpretation of reality. If I know, from of my own field experience and my own sketches, what I wish to express, the photo can be a very useful tool to reach my objective. I have a large amount of reference material in the form of slides and photos published in magazines and journals. In those cases when I have had to base an illustration solely on a photograph, the result has usually been a disappointment – when I have later seen the bird in real life.

It has been particularly important for me to photograph birds in the hand. In association with ringing, there is the chance to take photographs of passerines in the hand before they are released again. These close-up pictures of quite a large number of variant individuals of common species have been an important basic material for the field guides. I try to avoid painting birds in postures that the eye cannot perceive, but the limits of what we are able to perceive have been shifted thanks to photography. Frozen images of birds in flight would be impossible to create without the help of the photo's 'vision'. As an example, it is almost impossible to see single feathers on the wing of a flying passerine, but the wing can be frozen by the camera shot. So, to understand what I see vaguely and very rapidly in the field, I may require a distinct picture in order to decipher this. In this way, a bird-book illustrator may need to prise at and twist reality slightly so as to make it perceptible.

Studies of Tree Pipit *Anthus trivialis*, 30 August 1991 Water-colour 32x25cm

Bird drawn in the hand when caught for ringing

77

Tristram's Warbler *Sylvia deserticola*, 1990–91
From *Birds of Europe with North Africa and the Middle East*

Field studies of Cyprus Warbler,
Eilat, 19 February 1990
Pencil 21x14 cm

Cyprus Warbler *Sylvia melanothorax* and
Ménétries's Warbler *Sylvia mystacea*, 1990–91
Illustration for *Birds of Europe with North Africa and the Middle East*

Study from skin collection, 1990
Tristram's Warbler and Ménétries's Warbler
Water-colour 30x40 cm

79

My first 'Peterson', *Fåglar i Europa* with my own illustration of an Osprey stuck in About 1965

This aspiration always to base a picture on your own observations alone, does it not have its drawbacks, especially for species which you have encountered just a few times? Do you not run the risk of relying too much on what you yourself believe you have seen?

Yes, the risk is there. In some cases, the live bird which I drew was perhaps not representative of the species or plumage, or even incorrectly identified. The dark-phase Long-legged Buzzard in *Birds of the Mediterranean and Alps* was based on a beautiful buzzard which I saw in south Turkey, a bird which I sketched in careful detail. It was changed in the later large edition as it was, in fact, a Common Buzzard of the Levantine subspecies *menetriesi*. For that edition I painted an eclipse male American Wigeon *Anas americana* which I had observed and photographed with great enthusiasm on Victoria Island, in British Columbia. This bird was accompanying a largish group of full-plumaged adult males and females which undoubtedly belonged to this species; furthermore, our Eurasian Wigeon *A. penelope* is not normally found in this part of the

world. I realised at the eleventh hour, however, that it was in fact a Eurasian Wigeon: the picture was then already in proof, but I was able to withdraw it. My present Nutcracker is one of a rare breed, showing a white rump, which they should not have. I thought that it was a genuine mistake, but in one of my sketch books from 1972 I have drawn it just like that, and perhaps this erroneous picture become firmly etched in my mind. The list can be made longer.

All the new information you presented in your original five volumes had a limited readership. It is only when these books are put together into one large volume that you really reach a wide European audience. Was it your Swedish publisher who suggested a single, amalgamated volume, or was this something you planned yourself? Was this included in your thoughts from the very beginning?

The decision to produce the amalgamated version in the form in which it was later to appear came to me gradually. In the early 1980s, I was more interested in painting freely and in travelling. The publishers, however, wanted to combine the five parts into one volume. We therefore agreed just to bind them together as they were, without any major revisions.

When I then examined some of the plates I had published, I felt that they needed to be replaced by new ones, they were not up to standard. Knowledge of field ornithology had increased rapidly and major advances in field identification had taken place. I therefore decided, to a limited extent, to add new material and revise the old. The change from grouping birds according to habitat to, instead, a systematic arrangement came about gradually. As recently as 1986, the plan was to divide the volume into landbirds and waterbirds. Then I broke my leg in spring 1987, and had difficulty in painting. So, I sat and pondered, looked at the pros and cons of all possibilities, and came to the only

reasonable conclusion – to combine the books into one and present the species in strict systematic order. Only then did I realise the magnitude of the work which faced me.

A Field Guide to the Birds of Britain and Europe by Peterson, Mountfort and Hollom, which was published as long ago as 1954, was to become very significant in the development of field ornithology. Peterson's plates show all species set out in a similar way, easy to compare, and with arrows showing the specific features to be looked for on each species. Was Peterson an important source of inspiration and an important tool in your own field observations?

'The Peterson guide' was tremendously important to me. I always took it with me on the excursions of my teenage years. It was completely different from the books I had looked at earlier. Peterson's plates felt much more modern – it was like hearing The Beatles after having hummed along to the songs of one's parents' old popular artists. 'The Peterson guide' raised my horizon in the 1960s to include the bird life of the entire continent, away from a narrower and traditional Swedish or Nordic perspective. It was a new way of seeing, with a feeling of order, classification and directness. I think that most ornithologists relate to this strict arrangement. It communicates with a part of us which is concerned with the collecting and sorting of information – a legacy from Linnaeus that most biologists probably carry.

Warblers, 1990
Water-colour, gouache and pencil
Illustration for *Birds of Europe with North Africa and the Middle East*

Above:
Grasshopper Warbler *Locustella naevia*, juvenile in autumn.
Lanceolated Warbler *Locustella lanceolata*: left, juvenile in autumn; right, bird in early summer.
Pallas's Grasshopper Warbler *Locustella certhiola*, juvenile in autumn.
Paddyfield Warbler *Acrocephalus agricola*, juvenile in autumn.
Booted Warbler *Hippolais caligata*, bird in spring.
Pencil-drawing at bottom left: Olivaceous Warbler *Hippolais pallida*.

Your ability to combine pedagogic clarity, exactness of depiction, with an aesthetically appealing composition of the plates is often talked about in connection with your field guides. In a way, your pictures deviate from the stricter arrangement to which we have become accustomed in Peterson's plates.

It is always difficult to find a balance between 'readability' and suspense in a picture. An illustration should be easy to interpret. Sometimes, I have perhaps waived clearness in favour of an exciting design. My basic feeling is that a rigid arrangement of the birds side by side has a pedagogic value. For me, it has not been enough to depict a bird as simply a symbol of its species, showing the usual characters; it has to possess a certain element of life as well. This point about life is a central one, it is all about giving an impression of living creatures. It cay therefore sometimes seem necessary to allow a bird to turn its head a little, or raise its tail. With small changes compared with what is expected, the bird is perceived to have a will of its own, a reason for being in just that very place where it is painted. I simply cannot help doing this, even though my aim has been to show them all in the same posture.

When composing a plate, it is crucial that the animal/bird has a goal, or a direction, a natural reason for being there. The viewer should be allowed to assume that the bird came from somewhere and that it will fly off to another destination. One of the most common failings in wildlife painting is that the animal seems to have been pasted in. The picture is then dead. The shortcomings and the advantages of paintings are often listed in theories on early Chinese landscape painting. A flawed work called 'stream without a source' is presented in Jao Tzu-jan's 'twelve points to be avoided' (12th century). The same could be said about a bird without a story – it has to have done something the moment before!

Central to instilling life in the individual bird is the feeling that its eye can see. Just as with humans, the bird's eye is the first thing we meet and it therefore has to be painted life-like. Many bird-illustrators depict the reflection in the eye in rather routine fashion, with a white speck being used as a means of creating life. An eye is a small, curved lens that reflects the light around it. If the sun is shining, a distinct pale spot is usually seen; if it is cloudy, there is a paler half-circle broken by whatever is present against the sky. The various small details surrounding the eye, the way the bare parts enclose the eye, and the fine rings of tiny feathers, create individual expressions.

For me, the work becomes too dreary if I am not permitted to convey these individual expressions and situations, not allowed to work with light and movement. Each encounter with a bird reflects a unique occasion. It is often difficult to replicate jizz, a term used to describe a combination of general shape, impression and silhouette, unless one introduces atmospheric elements.

In an article in the RSPB magazine Birds, *you have tried to answer the question 'When is a bird at its most typical?'. And you liken the question to the hesitation in choosing which postcard of London one should choose to send home. Which one best represents the city? In other words, this is the same issue you are confronted with when deciding how to depict a bird: in which posture does a given bird species reveal most of its own character?*

'Each sketch or painted image contains more or less of personal interpretation, and this is the way it should be. If I were to depict the Bluethroat in one single picture, I would choose a view obliquely from behind, where the blue colour is only hinted at. Where I live I see Bluethroats on passage, and they are very unobtrusive. I often attempt to point out a Bluethroat, but usually nobody sees any blue. Surprisingly often they turn the breast away, but the birds' posture, body shape and the pale supercilium nevertheless give an invariable "Bluethroat character". The picture of a Bluethroat seen diagonally from behind can, moreover, represent both sexes and all races. In the uplands, however, in their breeding areas, it is just the opposite: here, the blue breast gleams like a translucent sapphire from the top of every clump of willows in the light nights of early summer, and all other characters become secondary.'

You met Roger Tory Peterson many times, both in Sweden and during your travels in America. How do you feel about his contributions now and what were your impressions of the man behind the work?

I saw Roger Tory Peterson firstly as an ornithologist and a popular educationalist. His books express to a higher degree a passion for birds than a fondness for painting them. He thus inspired me more in my work as a field-guide author than as an artist. From the 1980s until his death in 1996, we met regularly in connection with art exhibitions in the USA. His passion for birds and his constant desire to learn more went with him throughout his life. When we met, he never missed an opportunity to talk birds.

Peterson extracted those characters that were conclusive for field identification. He made this information easy to handle and visually useful for his generation of field ornithologists, those who had exchanged the gun for a pair of binoculars. Therein lay his greatness. He simplified and standardised the individual bird portrait rather than developing and expanding it.

Barbary Partridge *Alectoris barbara*
and Red-legged Partridge *A. rufa*
Illustration for *Birds of Europe with
North Africa and the Middle East*
Water-colour and gouache
35x26 cm

Gunnar Brusewitz,
Roger Tory Peterson and Lars
Gotland, July 1982

On the coastal meadows in Hamra, 1982
Photo: Staffan Lindbom

Up to the beginning of the 20th century, study of birds in wildlife cabinets or birds that had been shot formed the basic material for ornithological illustrations. Then the binocular arrived, making it possible to see birds at longer range, and today, with the aid of a telescope, even birds a great distance away can be studied in detail. You have, in a way, chosen a direction different from Peterson's schematic approach. It could be said that you complicate rather than simplify the image of a bird, both its appearance and the way we react to seeing it. Is this a result of the telescope?

When I was growing up, the generation before ours used a telescope only in exceptional circumstances. I remember, for instance, an excursion with Roger Tory Peterson one day in September 1984. He brought along his first modern telescope, a Questar, which we assembled together – 'a scope like the new hotshots have', as he expressed it. In *Watching Birds*, James Fisher wrote that telescopes can be of great use, but they are probably not worth the money unless you have a problem to sort out. This illustrates the suspicious attitude of his generation towards the telescope as a tool for ornithological studies.

The birdwatchers who in the 1960s and 1970s studied birds through the strong magnification of a telescope lens demanded new field guides, guides that were more detailed and complete with regard to different plumages and age classes. There was an clear demand for something new, and I think that many had thoughts about producing a new guide to Europe's birds. We felt strongly that we had 'a problem to unravel'.

You are saying that bird guides reflect the tools that were used to get close to the birds, from the gun via the binocular to the telescope? Your field guides, based on availability of a telescope, break with Peterson's binocular-based pictures in the same way as he in his day broke with the zoologists of the 19th century, who studied primarily shot birds, those killed with a shotgun.

If one wants to generalise, then there is a lot in this. Peterson's generation was the first to look at birds by using binoculars alone, the ones who demanded a simplified guide in which those crucial distinguishing characters, those visible at a distance in the field, were indicated. The pictures in my guides, as in many others published during the 1990s, are aimed at a generation of birdwatchers who, by using a telescope, have once again got even closer to the bird. Observers who want to be able to distinguish between a Little Stint in juvenile plumage and one in summer plumage, between different wheatears in autumn plumage, and to be able to age a Lesser Spotted Eagle.

Paradoxically, it may seem as if your field-guide pictures, in their richness of detail and proximity to the individual bird, are closer to some of the pictures of birds that were painted around the turn of the previous century.

The painter who impressed me more than anybody else during my work on the field guides was the Swiss artist Léo-Paul Robert (1866–1923), who was a contemporary of Bruno Liljefors. His bird portraits were re-produced in a small series of handbooks on birds by the Frenchman Paul Géroudet. In 1974, I had acquired a full set of these in an antiquarian bookshop in London. What appeals to me is Robert's soft and picturesque way of bringing out plumage and flight feathers and, not least, his life-like faces. Did he use newly shot birds, did he watch birds in the field or did he work from photographs? I don't know. Perhaps he caught birds and put them in a cage? The interesting thing is that it is in fact only his passerines in *Les Passereaux* I–III that have a real sensitivity to them, and it was probably towards them that his passion was directed. They show a perfect

Long-eared Owl *Asio otus*
and Eagle Owl *Bubo bubo*
Illustration for *Birds of Europe with
North Africa and the Middle East*
Water-colour and gouache
35x26 cm

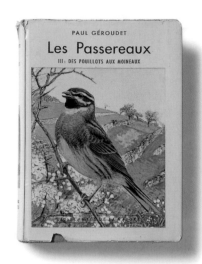

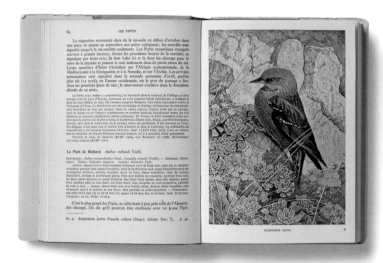

The book *Les Passereaux III* (1954) with
pictures by Léo-Paul Robert
Jacket: Cirl Bunting
86   Spread: Alpine Accentor

balance between vagueness and detail. They also contain many close-up studies of pieces of vegetation, for which Victorian water-colours could have been the source of inspiration. Robert frequently made use of gouache colours. His paintings of larger birds, the non-passerines, are more fabricated and in some cases are based entirely on photographic material, as they have a stiffer feel and radiate less warmth. In my opinion, the three volumes of passerines contain some marvellous portraits which are among the best that have ever been done. I have many times wondered how Robert acquired an awareness of all these small birds' facial patterns.

The second artist I have come to appreciate more and more is the American Louis Agassiz Fuertes (1874–1927). He is one of the artists who, when it comes to portraying birds, is perhaps my closest soul mate. He painted his birds mainly from subjects which had been shot. His treatment of feathers is innovative. He was one of the first to reproduce light and airy feathers which still have a structures and firmness. He shows, for example, how a tract of breast feathers stands out slightly because of the bird's posture, or how the scapular feathers form a physiognomic unit. He also has a very good feel for the rhythm in stripes and rows of spots, conjured up with apparently simple and obvious brushwork, something which looks easier than it actually is.

With Fuertes's wader pictures, I can see that they are done from freshly shot birds. It can be seen that the wings are a bit slack. The primaries are often slightly drooping and expose the secondaries, and the white wingbar of many species. This is seen only exceptionally on live waders; on a Dunlin, for example, a very distinct white wingbar is visible in flight, but it is concealed when the bird is at rest. But such an effect becomes permanent on a dried skin, and this misleading feature on waders has often been

depicted by subsequent illustrators. This is either part of the Fuertes legacy or an observation taken from the appearance of a bird skin.

The bird portraits by Fuertes tell us something about his keenness, his curiosity and wonder at what he saw before him. I can feel a strong sense of affinity with this. In the foreword to Abyssinian Birds and Mammals, a portfolio with a selection of his birds and animals from an expedition to Abyssinia in 1926–27, there is a description of his enthusiasm: 'That instinctive, inexplicable passion for birds which arouses an uncontrollable desire to know them intimately in their haunts and to make them part of our lives, and which overcomes every obstacle until, in a measure at least, this longing is gratified, is the heritage of the elect; and few have been more richly endowed than Louis Fuertes'.

The paintings by these two artists tell me something about their respective person-alities. Both have a humanistic streak, a humbleness towards what they have seen before them, a wonder and a deep feeling for the individual bird. This has inspired me.

Louis Agassiz Fuertes, 1927
African Scissor-tailed Kite *Chelictinia riocourii*
From *Album of Abyssinian Birds and Mammals*

Azure Tit *Parus cyanus* and Long-tailed Tit *Aegithalos caudatus*
Illustration for *Birds of Europe with North Africa and the Middle East*
Water-colour and 35x26 cm

The four Long-tailed Tits at the left represent the races:
europaeus continental Europe
rosaceus Britain and Ireland
irbii south Spain
tephronota Asia Minor

The two birds on the right are a *caudatus* from Scandinavia and northeast Europe, with nest in background, and a juvenile of race *europaeus*

Wilhelm von Wright:
Common Scoter, immature
male moulting to full plumage
From Lönnberg's edition of
the von Wright brothers' work
Svenska Fåglar 1929

The Finnish brothers Magnus, Wilhelm and Ferdinand von Wright hold a unique position in the Scandinavian tradition. During the first half of the 19th century they executed a series of paintings of mammals, birds, fishes, butterflies and other animals. Svenska foglar efter naturen på sten ritade *was published in the 1820s and 1830s. They belonged to a generation one step further back in time, and were thus contemporaries of Audubon. What is your relationship to the bird paintings of the von Wright brothers? Have they had an influence on you?*

When I started working on my books in the early 1970s their paintings were in fact a major source of inspiration. I felt that the von Wright brothers depicted real individuals, admittedly dead, but with an authentic plumage. The subjects were observed with an extremely sensitive eye and portrayed by an artist who was alive and interested. The birds were often depicted in somewhat unnatural postures, but were otherwise tremendously well done and detailed. The feet and bare parts were meticulously painted from freshly shot specimens. The pictures as a whole were to me, as a young man, slightly mysterious, perhaps fairytale-like, because of their old-fashioned stamp. The most obvious thing was

the scenery-like backgrounds, clearly done before the breakthrough of impressionism, which lent an historical feel to them.

During the 1920s, Einar Lönnberg produced a new edition of these masterpieces. The hand-painted lithographs of the first edition were transferred to zinc plates by skilled lithographers, together with a number of new plates made from unpublished water-colours by the brothers. These pictures were reproduced once more in a book by Gustaf Rudebeck published as recently as 1960, *Svenska Fåglar*. This indicates the status of the von Wright brothers in Swedish ornithological illustration.

Do these pictures still hold up today? Apart from the fact that they feel old-fashioned, has their scientific content not lost its importance?

The factual information was often remarkably exact, and always interesting. In my work I often referred to these books in the same way as one looks at a skin. I felt that they were reliable. If an immature male Common Scoter was depicted in first-winter plumage, I knew that just such an individual actually existed – their eye was unerring.

If one compares the originals from the 19th century with the plates in the later edition, it can be seen that somebody has made changes, in all cases with a negative outcome. This brings up the question of the artist's rights to his work, as well as the relationship between artist and author. The errors which are exposed when making comparisons are not due to shortcomings on the part of the lithographers, who are unquestionably highly skilled and meticulous. In those cases where they have been tasked with copying original water-colours the result is dazzling. Instead, these changes must have been the result of the author's ambition to update the almost hundred-year-old paintings.

In Lönnberg's 1920s edition, there are several paintings, including one of a Little Stint, which have been drastically altered from the original version. Professor Lönnberg presumably decided that the original lithograph did not correspond with modern knowledge and instructed somebody to update it. The result is instead a picture lacking in both artistic and scientific value. What was originally a unique observation by an artist's eye, which always has a validity, was converted and adapted according to the current scientific knowledge of the time. But whereas scientific 'truths' change, the unique observation is always timeless.

When, as a twenty-year-old, you embarked on the field-guide work, you were thus artistically in touch with these masters of the 19th century, at least the von Wright brothers through their work having been reproduced in more modern reference works. Did you have a general interest in the older tradition within the zoological literature?

When young, one is probably more interested in what is happening at the moment, at the time one can see. Also, as a young artist, you can easily be somewhat blinded by your own imagination and experiences, believing that you can see and perceive the world around you in a totally new way. And it has to be that way.

My interest in the historical aspect has grown over the years. When I now look back in time, in other words look at older pictures, I am often looking for two things. One is the factual content, the scientific facts that lie embedded in the picture. The other is the artist's presence in the painting. It is valuable if I think I can see what he was thinking or seeing or how he felt. In older works, however, both the information and what the artist is saying are often wrapped up in a dress typical of the period and which can be difficult to see through.

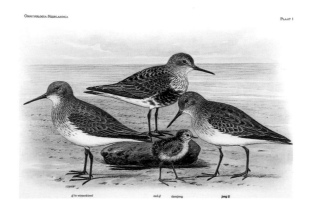

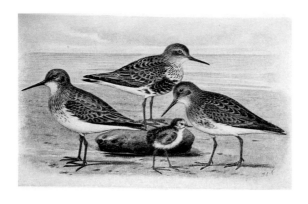

M. A. Koekkock: Dunlins
From Prof. Dr E. D. Van Oort's *Vogels van Nederland* (published 1925–26)

Below: same plate as above, but the bird in winter plumage at far right has been repainted as a juvenile
From H. F. Witherby *et al.* (eds.), *The Handbook of British Birds, vol. IV* (published 1940)

Wilhelm von Wright: Juvenile Little Stint
From *Svenska Foglar* (published 1828–1938)
Hand coloured lithograph

Below: same picture but partly overpainted
From Lönnberg's edition of the von Wright brothers' work *Svenska Fåglar* (published in 1920s)

89

When you read descriptions in older texts, can you find facts there which are relevant to our present-day knowledge and way of looking at things? You have studied one of the greatest pioneers in Swedish zoology of first half of the 19th century, Sven Nilsson. Beginning in 1820, he published a multi-volume work collectively entitled Skandinavisk fauna, en handbook för jägare och zoologer *[Scandinavian fauna, a handbook for hunters and zoologists]. Two volumes were devoted to birds.*

What is interesting and evokes my respect is always the observation made by the individual. During the 18th century and well into the 19th century, observations are characterised by the freshness of new discovery, sometimes spiced with romantic idealism. Authorities still hanging on to the ancient mythological legacy are called in question. The observer is free from prejudice at the same time as he contemplates the ingenious nature of God's creation. There is a wonderful sense of closeness in Gilbert White's or Thomas Berwick's observations, as well as in Nilsson's slightly more restrained prose. The museum ornithologist's comprehensive overview approach, scientifically more stringent but perhaps poorer in literary quality, appears in many works of the latter half of the 19th century.

When I read what Nilsson wrote on the Garden Warbler or Blackcap, for instance, I find several beautifully worded passages that point to the intrinsic poetry of observation. And what I feel is that some interpreters of nature carry their personal presence in text or picture. They create an encounter for those who are able to interpret the plain text or the evidently objective image. When I read Nilsson, I become somewhat lyrical at the thought of his capacity to observe, his care over the small details. But only through being able to relate to these details myself am I able to see traits of his personality.

When I studied Garden Warblers in the hand during ringing work in the 1970s, what I found was that they had some grey on the side of the neck. This was not shown in any of the guides in which I looked. But Sven Nilsson had seen it, he discovered the grey neck side of the Garden Warbler, something which I, too, thought I was doing 150 years later. And this mutual observation was not an established truth that had been etched into the reference works of standard knowledge, to be simply repeated in stereotype fashion, it had to be discovered anew. His obviously sharp eye describes the Garden Warbler:

> All upper parts of body brownish-grey with more or less noticeable olive-grey tinge / Across the sides of the neck an ashy-grey streak. / breast and sides pale grey with an indistinct rusty-yellowish tinge / remiges brown, outer edges of the same colour as the back, the tips paler.

In the first volume of *Fåglar i Naturen*, I wrote on the Garden Warbler's appearance:

> At first sight seems to lack any distinct features altogether, and at a distance the uniformly warm colour most recalls a Reed Warbler. But at close range a number of small details are visible which give the bird a certain character: fine-tuned nuances of colour with ochre belly sides and often mouse-grey neck sides / In fresh plumage the pale-tipped primaries are distinctive, especially when seen from behind.

This observation was lost, however, in the 1978 English translation, *Birds of Wood, Park and Garden*. I realise how easily information is misinterpreted before it has been incorporated into a generally accepted tradition of wording. The English text says: 'At close quarters however, there are delicate shades on ochre flanks and mouse-grey sides to the throat.' The phrase 'often mouse-grey neck sides' has become 'mouse-grey sides to the throat'.

Garden Warbler *Sylvia borin*, 1991
Water-colour and pencil 37x27.5 cm

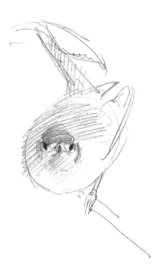

Study of Blackcap

The small nuances discovered by Nilsson's eye, and long afterwards by me, were not to be found in any of the books of the time, whether in the 1820s or in the 1970s. We thereby share an experience which, when I first read his words, for a brief second created a contact between us. The most reliable source when I embarked on my guides was *The Handbook of British Birds* (Witherby, Jourdain, Ticehurst & Tucker); my edition was revised in 1943, and these details were not mentioned there. Eliot Howard, another wonderful observer, does, however, mention in *The British Warblers* (1907–14) that the sides of the neck are somewhat 'Suffused with ash grey'.

Nilsson writes on the Blackcap:

The whole hood, from forehead through the upper part of the eyes to the nape, pure black, glossy. The sides of the head and neck together with the nape ashy blue. The eyelids are clad in short black down above, short white down below. Back, shoulders, wing-coverts and rump ashy grey with an olive-green tinge.

Following this, he notes the female as: 'The hood rusty-brown, the sides of the head and neck greyish; lacking the wonderful ashy-grey colour that adorns the male…'.

A serene and elegant observation that conveys not only scientific exactness but also a feeling, an insight into the author's aesthetic experience of the bird.

Do you feel that your relationship with nature and your maturity as an observer and interpreter of nature have distinct roots in a Swedish or Scandinavian tradition, rather than in the British or American one?

It is difficult to get a general view of or to reflect on my own relationship with tradition. There is, of course, a distinctly Swedish tradition, partly divorced from the British one, that has directly or indirectly influenced me. My interest in the British tradition in the initial stages of my work, however, most certainly stimulated it.

As for the texts in my field guides, all ornithologists of my generation and the immediately preceding ones have strong ties with the Swede Erik Rosenberg. It was generally considered that in *Sveriges Fåglar* he had described the Swedish avifauna so brilliantly that it could not be bettered. He was for ornithological wildlife prose what Liljefors was for wildlife-painting, impossible to avoid. Many Swedish authorities in recent centuries, however, have, as a result of language barriers and a widespread nationalism, remained known only in their own country. Linné, writing in Latin, was immediately recognised internationally for his work and created a European Linnaean tradition. With the birth of sovereign states in the 17th century and increasing nationalism, however, the language of learning, Latin, was gradually replaced by the respective country's own language. Linnaeus was, by the way, the first person to produce a national fauna for a single country: his *Fauna Svecica* was published in Stockholm in 1746. The strong tradition of national faunas that dominated publishing for 300 years was broken during the 1970s.

Symptomatic of this was the fact that the English version of my field guide was christened *Birds of Europe with North Africa and the Middle East*, as that title had not already been used. All English bird guides were traditionally given the name 'Birds of Britain and Europe' or something similar.

But your books have now been around for ten years. A couple of years ago, in 1999, a new, complete guide to Europe's birds by Svensson, Mullarney, Zetterström and Grant, the Collins Bird Guide, *was published. How do you see the future for bird guides? Is there a new generation of ornithologists in the making that will demand new books, taking new directions?*

It is probable, or maybe, rather, obvious. The question is simply what they will look like. The *Bird Guide* is an outstandingly good work which is consistently and systematically accomplished and with superb plates. But perhaps future field guides will be electronic and/or make use of artificially painted plates based on photographs. The first thing to happen is very likely to be the employment of a new systematic list, based on molecular-genetic research. The entire concept of what a species is is perhaps being broken apart, and we have a totally new direction to take. Birdwatchers are now talking about phylogenetic species, or determining from which population an individual stems. Maybe there will be a revival of Peterson, or maybe I shall be put in mothballs for 50 years only to be dusted off again later – 'look, there… Jonsson already wrote 70 years ago that the male Scaup in first-winter plumage had….'.

Of one thing, however, I feel certain – interest in birds and in the painted picture of a bird will endure!

Juvenile gulls, 1998
Illustration for article on field identification of large gulls
Water-colour 25x32 cm

Herring Gull *Larus argentatus*
Caspian Gull *Larus cachinnans*
'South European Gull' *Larus michahellis*

Feathers from mantle and scapulars
of Great Northern Diver *Gavia immer*
Illustration for *Lommar* (1992)
Gouache 32x25 cm

Above: juvenile, fresh and worn
scapulars and one small mantle feather;
on right, a mantle feather from first-
winter plumage
Centre: typical scapular feathers in
first-winter plumage, with variations
Bottom: two variants of scapular
feathers of winter-plumaged adult and,
at right, a scapular feather from first-
summer plumage with a dark scapular
from bird in second-winter plumage

Semipalmated Plover *Charadrius
semipalmatus* and Ringed Plover
C. hiaticula, 1996
Water-colour and pencil 23x32 cm

Pied Wagtail *Motacilla alba*
Illustration for *Birds of Europe with North Africa
and the Middle East*
Water-colour and gouache 10x17 cm

Top: juvenile of race *alba* and winter-plumaged
female of race *yarrellii*
Bottom: male of race *subpersonata* in summer and
in winter plumage

96

Black-eared Wheatear and
Pied Wheatear, 1989–91
Illustration for *Birds of Europe with North
Africa and the Middle East*
Water-colour and gouache 31x24 cm

Top: Black-eared Wheatear *Oenanthe
hispanica*, adult female of eastern race
melanoleuca and of western race *hispanica*,
with juvenile of eastern race; all in
winter plumage in September
Bottom: Pied Wheatear *Oenanthe
pleschanka*, young male with immature
and adult female in winter plumage in
autumn

Study of juvenile Tundra Gull *Larus vegae*
Coshi, Japan, 1 February 1999
Water-colour 25x32 cm

Mellanakt [*Intermission*], 1982
Ruff
Oil 80x130 cm

100

The work on the bird guide – which was to take almost twenty years of more or less intensive work – meant that, as you mentioned earlier, you had to shift your activity somewhat away from the more sustained experimentation with art. Art is there the whole time, but it does not take up a central position. But when the first edition of the five volumes is completed, in 1979, you virtually explode and throw yourself with great zest into painting. You enter into a kind of conversation with art, the classical masters as well as some of the 20th century art.

In retrospect, I can see that I did not have much time during the 1970s to go more deeply into the complexities of art. I did, admittedly, do some painting outside the context of the field guide, but thoughts or feelings that came to me could rarely be developed – they had to be suppressed because of new deadlines.

I therefore decided to spend the spring of 1980 in southern Spain. My bus was filled with painting equipment, telescope, camera, guitar and books on art. It was, in a way, my 'grand tour', even though my journey took me across the Pyrenees to Granada rather than to Venice.

In Spain I saw many beautiful landscapes that took a hold on me, landscapes that inspired me to paint. To see nature, to experience it and digest it is one thing, but to find a way to express the experience is another matter altogether. I had strong expectations that I would be able to express my experiences of the Andalusian landscape in traditional landscape painting, if I just worked intensively. I tried out the greyish-purple fig-tree branches against the reddish soil, the regular rows of olive trees, the bulls, the sun breaking through over the macchia and the bare mountains. I sketched every-thing, from the small black piglets in the mountains' oak forests to the cats at the

Fig tree, Sierra de Castillejos, 24 February 1980
Water-colour and red crayon 35x50 cm

Torremolinos refuse-tips. I painted both in water-colours and in oils. I painted in the field, with the subject in front of me, and then continued to work on the subjects in the apartment I had rented. But I found it difficult really to find myself in the subjects, to find a way of expressing my own self – well, perhaps it was there in the birds or in the bulls. Ferdinand, the bull which preferred to sit alone and sniff the flowers beneath the cork oaks, was my alter ego as a child.

I could alternate between times when I would think that everything I did was really good and other times when all painting felt quite meaningless. I was seeking something

that could be described as a true expression of myself, really to feel that I as an individual am present when I am painting. But is so easy to fool oneself, to believe that it is I who is seeing, while a van Gogh or a Monet finds its way into one's perception.

Young Andalusian Bull, 1980
Water-colour 26x56 cm

101

shallow water reflected a bluish-grey haze on the horizon and was strewn with white flowers. Groups of Little Egrets were standing there, White Storks promenading, elegant Whiskered Terns hunted over the water's surface and a group of white horses appeared and drank from the water. In the background the village was slowly awaking and a Spotless Starling could be heard squeezing out its song from its perch in a nearby old cork oak – I felt as if I had found Arcadia, or Paradise.

The picture was developed on the lines of a deliberate composition drawing on symbolism in a painting by Piero della Fransesca, 'Il batissimo di Cristo', as treated by Ulf Linde in his booklet *Geometrin i en målning av Piero della Francesca* [Geometry in a painting by Piero della Francesca] (Stockholm 1974). Piero's interest in mathematics and geometry finds expression in his paintings, which have a strict geometrical composition full of both religious and neo-Platonic symbols. The message in Piero's painting is that Christ receives divineness through his navel, and then fertilises the world with this divineness through his genitals. Christ is the spirit that can be inscribed into the regular pentagon, he is fertilised through the circle, symbolising God, being tangent at its lower edge to Christ's navel, and the earth, symbolised by the cube, has a centre that coincides with Christ's genitalia. I was thrilled by this deliberate way of composing a picture, and it happened to coincide with my own strong experience of 'divine beauty'. I saw the often strict and almost rigid composition in paintings from the Middle Ages and the early Renaissance as merely an expression of an architectonic form, adapted as a background to church altars.

When one wanders through the large halls of the Prado, which I did on my trip south, one is overwhelmed by the amount of art that has religious overtones – the extravagance in ornamentation and gold that one encounters in the catholic churches and the ever-present religious symbols, not to mention the large

One of the paintings you did in Spain that spring shows three white egrets in a marsh: you call it Andalusian morning. You showed it at a gallery exhibition in Stockholm in 1981, and you also sent it on your first participation in the exhibition 'Birds in Art' in Wisconsin in the following year. This painting has, I understand, been important to you. Did you find something of your own in it or does it symbolise itself your stay in Spain?

The painting of the Little Egrets came to mean quite a lot to me, maybe because it represents a thought or a process rather than a picture in itself. Come to think of it, it is perhaps one of the first paintings where I try to sort out the light conditions which exist around white birds in shallow water.

The studies and preliminary works are from Las Marismas in Andalusia, a 'divine' morning just outside the small village of El Rocio next to the famous Coto Doñana. The spring flood had created vast floodlands. The

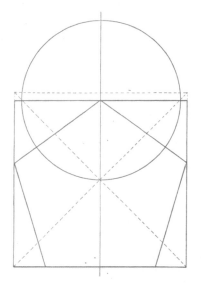

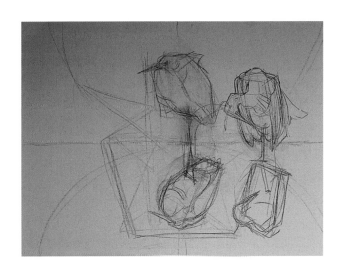

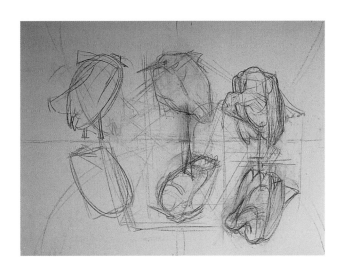

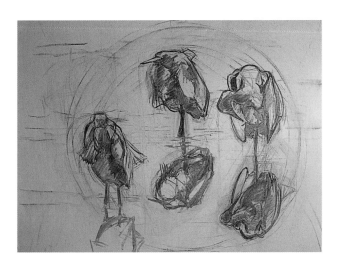

Analytical drawing of
Il batissimo di Cristo
From *Geometrin i en
målning av Piero della
Francesca* by Ulf Linde,
1974
*Piero della Francesca, Il
batissimo di Cristo*, ca 1458

Various attempts at
composition for
Andalusian Morning
Charcoal on canvas.
Torremolinos, 1980

103

Self-portrait
Andalusia, 1980
Oil 73x60 cm

Oak
Andalusia, 1980
Oil 92x73 cm

Easter processions in Malaga. All this made
me reflect over man's seemingly futile search
for God. The feeling I got that morning at El
Rocio was that it is only here, on our own
earth, that we can find the heavenly element,
or something that can be likened to a God. I
therefore made the three geometrical shapes
fall together. I tried to work my three birds
into the same circle and also to have the birds
marking out the regular pentagon and the
cube.

The result of my ruminations over this
picture was, for all that, that composition is
important, that the underlying geometrical
relationships are often critical for the reading
of a picture, not only its literary content, but
also its emotional readability. That thoughts
surrounding the construction of pictures are
seated in the colour itself. There is no divine
geometry needed for this, but a conscious
consideration for proportions.

*During this period you also painted several images
of cats on a refuse-tip. Are these an expression of the
idea that not only heaven but also the underworld
can be observed in this, our world? In a larger
painting, a cat with turquoise-green eyes is staring
at somebody casting a shadow over the refuse.
What is the idea behind this?*

The background is actually quite simple.
Around the area where I lived on the
outskirts of Torremolinos, there were many
wild cats that prowled about, feeding on
refuse and catching small birds. I started
sketching these and became fascinated by
their physiognomy. Many were malnourished
and looked quite hideous. When I passed a
demolition site in the village which had been
turned into a dump for tourists' refuse, it was
full of these cats. I started to sketch them.
And I noted a distinct social interplay between them. Because I was there drawing in
my sketchpad, passers-by also began to
become interested. At first, this was just an

irritation to me, but I soon started to wonder
what function my eye actually had – what I
looked at attracted others to look for. My
watching the cats caused more people to look,
either in an attempt to understand what it
was I was looking at or to pity the animals.
One boy with his mother stood and watched
for a long time until he saw the rubbish as an
opportunity, when he jumped over the fence
and picked up some empty bottles (unaware
that they could not be returned for money).
His mother quietly accepted this at first, then
actively pointed – there's one more – and
finally was brusquely admonishing when he
started to lift up rubbish in his search for
more bottles, and several other bystanders
watched with disgust. It became a complicated assortment of watching people, where
everybody looked with a different eye, just
because I had started to sketch a pregnant
grubby cat.

The cat looks up at a human, an adult
who does not see the cat but points out

104

Cat and refuse, 1980
Oil 130x88cm

something else to his child, who does not see what he sees. After a while I myself became interested in the rubbish, in the environment as a picturesque subject. I found that the brown and grey tones, the chequered butter pack and cans, were exciting to paint. The literary content was for me an amusing side issue; my interest lay in examining and capturing the nature of things, investigating their possibilities in terms of painting.

A third painting, which I know to be an expression of your dialogues with art during this period, is a rather hastily done self-portrait with the statement: 'If aestheticism is for the artist what ornithology is for the birds, then I don't give a damn for aesthetics, for birds do not give a damn for ornithology – I paint, they fly'. This is perhaps a contradictory statement from somebody who works as an artist – do you not care about aestheticism?

The picture was quite spontaneously done, but it hangs in my studio and I have come to like it. The statement is a comment on or dialogue with strict aesthetics which the American artist Barnett Newman (1905–1970) represented. I became fascinated with his pictures for one simple reason: he was both an active ornithologist and an artist at the same time, without expressing this in his art – or has he done this in a veiled way? He made the statement 'Aestheticism is for artists what ornithology is for birds'. The question I asked myself was how strong an influence the current aestheticism has on the individual artist. He thought that, in his painting, the choice was between 'nature and geometry'. He sought a middle-of-the-road approach. Are his strictly geometrical paintings actually a suppressed desire to paint a Red Cardinal, a Scarlet Tanager or a Northern Oriole? When I first came to the USA, in autumn 1981, it struck me what strong red colours, what an explosion of intensive red, many North American birds show. My stay in the USA included my first

encounters with the American avifauna and the paintings in the Museum of Modern Art.

I tried to analyse Newman's statement and came to the conclusion that maxims of this type, which artists love to utter, do not actually say much, they can be interpreted in any way. And maybe that is the purpose of them – just like art – I like lingonberry jam! Similar statements rarely stand up to philosophical analysis: they are more about painting than philosophy, more a means of expressing the addition of mysterious dimensions rather than clarification.

Ornithology is the science dealing with birds, which is a human notion and totally irrelevant for the birds in their daily lives. They do not fly because ornithology describes them as flying creatures. The question is whether Newman painted his images for the

same reason as the birds fly, which probably was his aim. He saw history of art as something which stood between him and 'the origin of the sense of tragedy'. He wanted to achieve some kind of original, primal feeling. The question is whether it was in fact not the history of art that stood between him and the birds, that it was aestheticism rather than 'the primordial [tragic] feeling' that moulded his painting. I was quite willing to believe that, and therefore I was willing to deny the aesthetic dogma that tried to govern what I should paint, hence this declaration. In no way does this imply that I dislike Newman's pictures. In his rigid panels of red and black or white there is a 'live' edge that flutters, a trapped bird perhaps.

Scarlet Tanager, 1995

Autodidakt, 1982
Oil 80x80 cm

At your large exhibition at the Natural History Museum in Stockholm in 1984, which was something of a breakthrough for you, there was a painting of three Avocets from Gotland. It has a colour range which seemed new, it has more of a Nordic light, the birds are sharply turquoise while the water is bright yellow. It seems to indicate a new light or a new scale of colours. Earlier, your oil-paintings at least were based mainly on shape and brushwork.

Most of my oils from the early 1970s perhaps lack a distinct colour treatment. They have partly the colour range of the water-colour and perhaps even more a brushwork that is reminiscent of that of the water-colour. During the later part of that decade I tried to find a more picturesque form, but I did not get that far – the books demanded my attention. I had realised in 1980, in Spain, that the essential character of an oil-painting

differs from that of a water-colour. During the summer months of 1981 and 1982 I did a lot of painting in water-colours on the beach on Gotland, which resulted in the book *Ön*, published in *English as Bird Island, Pictures from a Shoal of Sand*. I was on the beach in all conceivable kinds of light, and maybe that was when I discovered something in the light. This painting originates from when I was sleeping on the small islet, as I describe in the book. In the morning, immediately before sunrise, I saw an Avocet against the light which somehow revealed these colours. And I made a water-colour sketch on the spot, lying in my sleeping bag on the sand.

The picture was composed later in the studio. My thoughts surrounding the Little Egrets are also present in this picture, but now it was all about my own place on earth – the beach on Gotland. I cannot state that I deliberately sought a strictly geometric

construction, but it came to express a series of geometric relationships.

The yellow water at the foot of the picture relates to the upper strip in the same way as the dark sand relates to the reflection of it, two in one. The same applies to the relationship between the birds, two and one. The picture has basically three fields of colour, and this trinity – water, earth and air – is repeated in the three birds. Relationships that interlock, are repeated and mirrored in the water. Through these simple elements consisting of some birds, a beach and water I was able to express myself.

Sunrise
Avocet, August 1981
Water-colour 51x36 cm

Treenighet [Trinity], 1983
Avocets
Oil 110x120 cm

Travelling still takes up a large part of your life after the work on the field guides is completed, but at the same time Gotland, its wildlife and the beach and meadowlands around your home become more and more important in your world of ideas. In three books having more the of a diarial – or even literary – character, Bird Island *(1983),* En dag i maj *(1990) and* Dagrar *(2000) – which can be considered a Gotland trilogy – it is the landscape around your house and your studio that is the focal point. Can you explain what it is in the Gotland landscape, its fields and sea, that attracts you? Why is this your place on earth?*

The question of how one finds 'his' or 'her' landscape is in many ways difficult to answer. Gotland has become my landscape. Since I spent my childhood summers on the Gotland coast, it is perhaps natural that this is where I feel most comfortable, most at home. Just how a landscape slowly takes possession of you, and you finally feel at home in it, is a question that one can ask oneself.

One of the most important features of this area is the mule-grazed littoral meadows with their richness of waders. Here there is also the more barren steppe-like *alvar* landscape, with its combination of heath vegetation and rich deciduous forests. Maybe it is the mix of these different cultural environments that gives the landscape its character. The openness of the landscape is, however, more important than anything else. The unhindered view of the horizon makes another way of thinking possible, the imagination can in a way be let loose. Sometimes it feels as if perspectives in the external topography of the land influence the internal landscape. When I travel abroad, I find myself attracted to landscape which have a similar structure to that in which I live: the prairies of North America, the tundra of Siberia or other vast open grasslands, steppes and semi-deserts inspire me more as an artist than do, for example, wooded landscapes.

I am convinced, however, that, as an

artist, one seeks a landscape of one's own, a landscape in which to reflect oneself and which eventually becomes a part of oneself, one's character.

In the book Bird Island*, you give an account of the animal and bird life during one summer on a small sand shoal in a small inlet on the Gotland coast. In your account, you follow intimately and in scrupulous detail what takes place that summer from what I should like to call the birds' perspective – even the young bulls that stray out on to the islet are obseved from the birds' point of view. There is only one passage in the book where humans turn up:*

> Far off there is a light shining in a window. Some secluded cottage where summer guests are playing some game? – there's no way I can know. Maybe somebody is sitting on the doorstep enjoying the fragrance of jasmine, and pulling a shawl around the shoulders when the first cool air of twilight makes itself felt. It looks cosy in any case, but we in the bay are in another world where a thousand fish eyes, a dozen herons and I are trying to make the most of the night.

What made you to want to write this book, and was the perspective obvious from the beginning?

I had found a place for painting not far from our house, right out on a small headland next to a shallow sea inlet. I could sit there against a stone wall and look out over the bay, which

has a fabulous bird life. I painted with water-colours, sat there for most of every day with my dog Columbus, and looked and painted indiscriminately.

After a while, I had produced a series of water-colours which I felt went together, which were in a way interdependent, and the idea for the book *Bird Island* was born. The perspective itself, which is indeed partly that of the birds, I never thought about.

Columbus, 1981
Water-colour 31×46 cm

Stilla kväll [*Tranquil evening*], 1981
Ringed Plover
Water-colour 36x47.5 cm

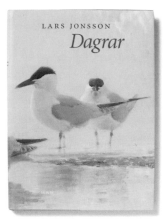

In the second part of the Gotland trilogy, En dag i maj *[A Day in May], a new perspective has crept in: Ragnhild and you got married in 1985, and you have had three children and you now find yourself in the centre of a social situation. You describe how people telephone you, you talk about breakfast arrangements and how the cucumbers ought to be replanted in the greenhouse. It seems that there are other things than just you and the birds. One gets a feeling that you are in a gret hurry to capture the instant moment.*

You write at last light, just before the approaching nightfall:

An almost full moon, pale yellow. Recognise myself in this last trembling light, how the senses and the brush wrestle with time, how one scoops the water of life from a bucket running dry, how one sees the sunlight slowly run out of one's hands and how much one would like to keep it there.

And in the last part, Dagrar, *you are sat painting down by your bay when the air is suddenly filled with red ants swarming around you.*

They do not bite, nor do I think they are a nuisance. They represent a crescendo of a lifecycle and are mixed with enormous clouds of midges, which hum and buzz like rushing water in distant pipes. When I look out over the dry grassland towards the setting sun, the swarming insects look

like mist. Occasional waders call, a heron lands in the distance, but the stillness is overpowering.

The back of my neck is soon full of winged ants, and the young Spotted Redshank so beautifully posed and which I had intended to draw is pushed aside by a Lapwing. I am uncertain whether I can catch up with time, it seems as if the evenings slip out of my hands, float away without my being there – other than as a bystander.

It is, of course, dangerous to overinterpret notes that are strongly tied to particular moments. But even so, in these quotations I cannot help but detect a feeling for life, where the early clear identification with the birds, nature, slowly deepens and becomes a realisation of being an outsider also in the presence of nature.

What I was thinking in the piece on the red ants, about not being present, is a condition that is often evident to me, that there is a difference between being present as a painter and being present only as an observer. That evening I could enjoy the landscape, but I was not part of the landscape I saw in front of me, I was not one with the evening. Perhaps it is about what is normally termed inspiration, being taken up in an activity that fills you completely, when the notion of time is erased. This is not, of course, unique to an artist, but perhaps more common, to be absorbed in a creative process.

But I assume that you mean the change that takes place in my relationship with the subject, that it is an expression of a maturity, from being a bird to becoming a human being, yes, perhaps. It is clear that these books span a twenty-year period, and a lot of things happen in one's life. We have an ability to close our eyes to what goes on inside us. We see ourselves as the same person mentally as when we were younger, but those around us see the changes.

For this book I have had reason more than ever before to reflect over what has happened over the years and what the driving forces behind my creativity are, how they constantly change and how the perspectives shift to an extent. My strongest feeling, however, is, perhaps somewhat frighteningly, how little actually changes. I can recognise myself in thoughts which I had as a teenager, I think I see the same things.

Can it be that case that I continuously ask myself the same question, what it is in birds that attracts me?

Of course, I changed over these years, and my family naturally becomes the focal point in my life, around which most things revolve. I must admit, however, that the side of me that is concerned with myself and my relationship to nature has a specific communicative space of its own somewhere. This is something which to a great extent goes back to experiences in my childhood.

Pied Flycatcher and apple blossom
May 1989
Water-colour 42x56 cm

Painting sea otters
Monterey, California, November 1986

Ragnhild and Martin looking at a
ground-squirrel

114

*If Gotland is the permanent, ever-present landscape
to which you always return, then your place on
earth is also to a high degree that of the traveller.
You travel a great deal in North America during
the 1980s. In the spring of 1984 you follow the birds
on their northbound migration over the North
American continent, from Florida in the south to
the Bering Straits in the Arctic. And together with
Ragnhild and Martin, then 16 months old, you
drive along the west coast in autumn 1986. You also
take part in the American art scene. From 1982,
you are a regular exhibitor at Leigh Yawley Woodson
Art Museum in Wisconsin, in its annual exhibition
'Birds in Art'. In 1987, you become the youngest
person ever to receive its award 'Master Wildlife
Artist'. Was this a conscious move to seek a new
landscape, or was it a new market attracting you?*

It was probably the birds that attracted me,
especially the American waders. There was also
the culture, with many wildlife artists, that
inspired me. I became acquainted with a large
number of people thanks to my bird guides,
and was accepted in new circles. The Swedish-
born sculptor Kent Ullberg and Roger Tory
Peterson were instrumental in this.

It takes time to become comfortable in a
new landscape. Even if one can make good
paintings at the first encounter, time is
needed for the relationships with the
landscape and its fauna to mature. When I
get to know an environment, my understanding of it deepens and I find sounding
boards for myself in the material life outside.
That part of painting where I can establish
contact with my own dreams and feelings
becomes more interesting, at least for myself.
Maybe that is why all landscapes which I have
visited and enjoyed for their colour show
similarities to Scandinavia when it comes to
light and certain vegetation structures.

FROM THE DIARY, 7th-17th NOVEMBER 1986,
IN MONTEREY, CALIFORNIA.
How to sum up the time in Monterey? There
is only one label to stick on it, OTTER,

Operation Otter. Apart from the first few
days when seabirds got their share of my
attention, otters have overshadowed the rest
of the time. Eventually it became an
obsession: as soon as I closed my eyes I saw
otters, big sulky faces, like thick-furred
puppies. The main feature was centred
around the expression itself, the mounds and
hollows that shape and sculpture the face –
hellishly difficult! It is not made any easier
by trying to check everything now and then
through the Questar [telescope] at some 100
metres' distance – often bobbing up and
down in the swelling waters as well. I bought
all postcards of otters I could lay my hands
on and took two rolls of Kodachrome film,
which I sent for express developing. But took
photos only of animals fishing near the
beach, dripping and in no way resembling
the teddybears sleeping farther out in the
kelp. Went back to the aquarium once more,
but this time they were all mostly under
water. On the final day, half-an-hour before
dark, I discovered a pair plus a half-grown
young floating in kelp in the harbour.
Frantically photographed and watched as
darkness fell. We stopped there again on the
last morning, and the real highlight came
when I managed to attract attention from an
older couple in a dinghy who had just
photographed them close to. They allowed
me to come out with them to one of the
lures, and I shot a roll and a half at down to
five metres – what a feeling!

Painted 7-8 water-colour studies plus 2
oils on the spot. Nothing perfect, but still an
important basis for future work.

Mostly sunshine during the days, and
Martin and Ragnhild could spend the time
on the beach and sunbathe a bit – it felt
wonderful.

Ljuset av en grå dag [*The light of a grey day*], 1986
Sea otter
Oil 112x120 cm

Water studies from the
expedition vessel during
Tundra Ecology expedition,
summer 1994

Barents Sea
11.30 hours 7 June 1994
12.30 hours 7 June 1994

116   Water-colours 36x51 cm

19.30 hours 7 June 1994

Vandraren [The wanderer], 1995
Polar bear
Oil 200x380 cm

During the 1990s, Siberia and the tundra landscape also enter as an important ingredient in your world of painting. You make several expeditions to Russia. The trips are, of course, undertaken in connection with bird studies, but do they also satisfy other needs? In your books you talk with great empathy and warmth about the migrating birds which pass your bay. As in Bird Island, *when you write: 'I can distinctly feel the suction, the draught, when twelve Grey Plovers in hurried flight describe a perfectly straight line southwestwards across the afternoon sky.'*

To a large extent yes, and above all the trips to Siberia. These tundras have held a strong attraction for me since my childhood. An important part of this attraction is the many waders which stop off here on their autumn and spring migration, birds which breed in these remote regions. In all years when I have seen them stopping off here, it has felt as if they were carrying a bit of the tundra with them, a cryptic message encoded in their plumage. The annual migrations of birds touch on us as humans, perhaps we have a seed of restlessness in us that surfaces when we see these flights – I can feel that – suddenly, you long for another place.

In 1994, you took part as artist in the expedition Tundra-Ecology 1994, a joint Swedish and Russian scientific expedition following in the wake of A. E. Nordenskiöld. At that time it was the ship Vega that in 1887–88 managed to reach the Pacific Ocean via the Northeast Passage. Now you were travelling with a larger research vessel which could carry helicopters, with which you all landed on the tundra for scientific work. The Swedish Polar Research Secretariat has, since some 15 years ago, adopted the old practice of taking along an expedition artist. In the old days, the artist was supposed to record the new places, different cultures, ethnographic objects and natural phenomena that were encountered: he was an important part of the documentation process. What can an artist document that other specialised instruments, photo and video, cannot?

Maybe the idea of this venture is to add another pair of eyes, different from those which science represents. The simplest answer to this is that the artist can document that which the scientists do not see, those values that cannot be described by advanced measuring equipment. Everything from social interactions on the ship to the music of the ice or the reaction of the individual when encountering the polar ice. The artist's perhaps somewhat unconventional angles of approach can, one hopes, bring something extra to the scientific outlook, too.

On this expedition, I myself gained a better insight into the scientific way of thinking, which has several parallels with the artistic way. To try to interpret the world around us, to see how things relate to each other, and how we often are governed by preconceptions; questions like these occupy science and art alike, but our methods of dealing with them are often different.

Since I have myself approached the field of scientific research in my work with birds, I can clearly detect the similarities. The research into large gulls which I have pursued during the 1990s has been influenced in many ways by the impressions I got during the expedition in summer 1994. When I paint, it is often the rapid associations that constitute the very driving force in the decisions I take. It is just like opening a large number of drawers of information at the same time, and making associations freely between them, not letting one's thoughts be led down pre-termined paths. In the same way, I have experienced some memorable moments of clarity in my own rather sprawling research on large gulls. After much methodical work in systematically collecting data, sorted out into drawers or, rather, excel datasheets, pictures suddenly appear through associations when all information 'has come to the surface of one's consciousness'. The feeling that the scientific world can describe in different ways is, to some extent, of the same character as the one present in the creation of pictures.

In any case, I was fully charged up for this trip, both as a painter and as an ornithologist. Every day, indeed, every hour of the day, was tremendously intense. The light was present day and night, and it was difficult to sleep. The tundra landscape, the open flat or billowing tundra with its rich life of lemmings, birds and animals, is one of those places that have come closest to my soul.

On 5th August, I am sitting on the vast tundra on the Sjirokostan peninsula, north-east of the Yana river, after having seen a Snowy Owl mobbing a Wolf, and I write:

Parad i Karahavet [*Parade in the Kara Sea*], 1995
King Eider
Oil 110x180 cm

119

Study of singing Pine Warbler
Dendroica pinus, Myles Standish,
Massachusetts, May 1995
Pencil 27x20 cm

In Siberia one can see the earth's curve, so vast is the perspective.

Who seeks the tundra, somebody who is restless, searching within himself, who, protected by the endlessness, feels secure, the expansion, the pressure from within obtains a point of reference without limits and the soul can be at peace.

The places you have visited and, most of all, Gotland have been documented in your sketchbooks, which are also, to a large extent, your diaries. Your Gotland trilogy indeed emanates from notes and sketches made in these books. Earlier, when we talked about your field guide, you describe the sketch as the focal point in your method of working, in your way of approaching the individual bird. When we look around in your studio, there are sketchbooks everywhere. And especially during your Siberia trips, when the conditions for outdoor painting are very limited, the portable sketchbook is an important instrument.

The sketchbook is everything. A sketchbook must be free and without any ambitions, it must not put demands on you. There has to be many pages in it, so that an unsuccessful sketch can just be left in place for the next attempt on a clean page. Four out of five sketches or water-colour studies I do in the field are just initial attempts, unsuccessful or broken off when the bird flies away. To sketch is to train oneself in drawing and looking. You must never approach the sketchbook with the objective of making good sketches, this is pointless. Sketches done from photos or one's own paintings, they are not sketches but drawings.

Before the east Siberian trip in 1999 I had water-colour paper bound into sketchbooks. The paper is double-sided, one side with a relatively coarse grain suitable for water-colours and the reverse side with a smoother surface. On the smooth side one can make notes and more detailed sketches or water-colours. These books have since then become one of my most important tools, both when I am travelling and immediately I go out with binoculars. Before these books I had only ordinary sketchbooks, where I just did sketches or made notes, and water-colour paper, loose or in a block beside me. I still have plain sketchbooks of a simpler sort that I use in my gull studies, where both field observations and notes on museum skins are entered.

The diary or, rather, the notes during the day, are a kind of sketchbook of thought. When I was growing up, simple diary-writing was, as for many teenagers, a conversational partner. I cannot say that I regularly keep a diary today, a routine for writing about the 'day just gone'. In my sketchbooks I keep notes on birds: observations, moult in waders and gulls, notes on calls, minor incidents or behaviours which I observe and find interesting enough to jot down. There can also be comments around an idea for a picture in the form of a rudimentary sketch of a landscape or an indication of how the shadow fell. The commonest note, however, is of a purely ornithological nature:

> 'Lapwing
> Juv crest, scratchy, wretched, unsteady
> 1 ind. juv plumage but full-grown, seems
> to have one new scapular?
> 4-5 scapulars with purple gloss
> no blue gloss on the wing'

Normally, there is no specific purpose attaching to these notes. I have in mind that they may be of use some day. In my case, however, I have throughout my life had various projects on the go, different books or current or projected papers on small waders, large gulls, divers, or moult in Wigeons or Scaups. The book is always present in the back of my mind. But the driving force behind note-taking is probably just as much a tradition, an ornithological culture that does not necessarily have to be used for a specific purpose.

Sketchbook: Studies of female Pintail, Hamra, 2000

Sketches of birds occupy most pages, and in those notebooks that are not suitable for painting in the sketch is often followed by notes about colours or light as an aid to memory. If the vision has given a stimulus for a painting, when the subject is encompassed by an atmosphere, a short comment can help to compose my thought. A sketch of a Hooded Crow, sitting in a furrowed field, on 5th April 1991, is followed by these brief lines:

> Crow in evening light
> haze, grey field
> calm, contemplating
> the Redwing sings in the spinney

121

Ducks in mist
Aurriv, 13 October 2001
122   Water-colour 32x50 cm

The water-colour has long been one of your obvious ways of expressing yourself. In your early water-colours you follow a tradition, basically a British one, of making a detailed pencil drawing on to which you wash colours. At the beginning of the 1980s you seem to have found another technique, more open in character, which exploits more the interplay between water and colour. This more flowing form with which you depict the play of light among shorebirds and water has become something of a trademark for you. How did you come about developing this form?

It has actually developed gradually over the years through my sitting outdoors and painting with the subject directly in front of me. The mobility of birds has also forced me to work quickly and fluently. The sketch-like or more fluid work comes about when it is damp outside and I am in a hurry. I then found that the more dissolved water-colour catches the light and the birds' ethereal character better.

Water-colours in its purest form is in many respects similar to the Zen Buddhists' relationship with ink wash-drawing; with an accomplished technique and a total spiritual presence, the individual spontaneously expresses the present moment. There is no distance between the artist and the object. The artist is his own motif when he spontaneously allows his hand and brush to become one with his thought. I recognise myself in this 'dissolving' of the ego, the 'me'. When water-colour painting is at its best, there is no friction between hand and eye, it feels as if I disappear into the act itself.

It is largely about orchestrating what happens by chance. Working wet on wet means assessing exactly what stage the surface is at, applying the next colour when the underlying colour is exactly as moist as required to get the desired effect. The combination of the amount of water, the structure of the paper and the brushstrokes is often more important than getting an exact colour tone. These stages come to me almost instinctively, there is no time to think, and then the moment has already gone. It is like playing a piece of music: once you have got started there is only one way to go – onwards. I work to a rhythm and a melody, and what I see in front of me is a score.

Many of the experiences I have acquired through painting in the presence of nature, sinking into or becoming absorbed by nature, have been difficult to put into words. When I later came across certain statements on art made by Chinese writers, I felt strong points of contact. Some of the conditions which I had put into words myself suddenly seemed to be part of a larger experience.

Expressions that I had begun to use, such as 'the self-evident' and 'dissolving', are also found to a large extent among the Chinese landscape-painters. Kuo Hsi (c. 1020–1090) pointed out in The Great Message of Forest and Streams that 'most important is the complete detachment from disturbing outward conditions and a profound tranquillity or emptiness of the mind', which is 'a pre-condition for the painter's self-identification with the soul of his motive'.

In the water-colour, the pigment is distributed, is mixed and is laid down in a natural way. All life is based on fluid carrying with it building blocks which are divided out according to certain prescribed codes or physical laws. The water-colour therefore becomes alive in its nature if water is allowed to deposit the pigment, to leave it as a sediment over the coarse-grained sheet of paper. This feeling that nature itself has made an imprint, that one is only a docile medium for the laws of nature, creates a strong sense of affinity with nature. Oil-paint is less free-flowing in character, and in this case the imprints have to be created.

Life delineates itself on the canvas called time; and time never repeats, once gone forever gone; and so is an act, once done, it is never undone. Life is an ink painting, which must be executed once and for all time and without hesitation, without intellection, and no corrections, and no corrections are permissible or possible. Life is not like an oilpainting, which can be rubbed out and done over time and again until the artist is satisfied. With the ink painting any brush-strokes painted over a second time result in a smudge; the life has left it.

Dr D. T. Suzuki (1932)

The fleeting, irreversible moments to which Suzuki gives expression I see as the strength of the water-colour, those parts that have come into being seemingly without thought in an immediate and direct brushwork.

Paradoxically, the spontaneous and momentary requires meticulous preparations. Improvisation occurs only when in complete control of the technique. One has to work powerfully, clearly and without hesitation while the final result 'may have the appearance of some light touches thrown down at random' (Kuo Hsi). It is, in principle, impossible consciously to create the feeling of spontaneity. In the same way as the spontaneous and direct is an expression of, yes, why not spirit, the arranged spontaneous and the consciously 'temporary' are, in my eyes, an expression of lack of spirit.

Therefore, it is difficult to lie with a water-colour painting.

Vila i upplösning [*Rest seen with dissolved mind*], 1991
Black-headed Gull
Water-colour 42x56 cm

125

Some of your water-colours seem, quite contrary to this, to have taken a very long time to do. They are characterised by tremendous care and precision and less by spontaneous brushwork. Are these different ways of working with water-colour an expression of different purposes or governed by the character of the subject? The Woodcock on the forest floor, for example, with its complex pattern of dried plant parts and sprouting herbs, demands a different technique from the bird resting on a sunlight-drenched rock.

Both yes and no, and the water-colour is able to express different character traits in the artist. It is suitable both for a controlled, methodical chiselling-out of details and for spontaneous sketches, expressions that can be found within one and the same person or form part of a developmental process. In the careful building-up of colour washes in a complicated and detailed work there must be areas with a distinct water-colour character. Those parts of a water-colour that seem to have been produced by chance, with the help of the water, are in many respects its very soul. It is these parts that invite interpretation. The consciously and more technically applied colour makes up the skeleton which, so to speak, props up or supports the chance element, much like the ring required to create a soap-bubble. This, the technical part, can make up 90% of the work itself and the visible surface of the water-colour, but in my view it will remain soulless without the chance element.

Time is always a factor when I paint outdoors with a bird as the subject. The feeling that I am working in a race against time is a tangible one. While it can be pressurising it is at the same time also concentration, it forces me to be totally present in the moment, in the moment of execution. The moment I have captured consists of course of different pictures, different visual sensations that reach me through the eyepiece of the telescope during a period of time, in other words strata of short moments which become layers of wash. The present moment expressed as layers of time.

I can never watch through the telescope for a while and then paint for a period of several minutes. Each addition to the painting has to be preceded by a visual impression. I may, of course, interrupt my presence in front of the subject and look at the painting, analyse it and paint from the experience and visual impressions I have. But this is a completely different process from the one that takes place with the subject directly before my eyes.

There seems to be a limit to what we call the immediate short-term memory, seven or eight seconds I think the writer and neurologist Oliver Sachs stated, after which the impression is stored in the memory. When we later retrieve it from the memory to write it down or draw it, it has already been coloured by all other memories, by all other associations. When I look at something intensively with a view to 'painting it' or 'noting impressions', I focus on the subject for a few seconds and then turn my eyes to the paper and sketch a few strokes, look up at the subject again, study it, sketch, look up again, in a rhythmic interaction. I have never timed it, but it feels as if it is within this very timespan – when the short-term memory is activated – that the sketch becomes a true expression of the immediate vision.

The situation I am thinking of when I talk about 'dissolving' is when the visual impression never has time to become formulated into a thought, never has time to be set down as an idea in the memory, but is used without being coloured by earlier experiences. If one paints from memory, then the hand is guided by an experience already assimilated, not by the impression of the moment or, perhaps more correctly, the immediate first-hand impression. The key to the experience of what is seen is in the sketch: it contains more than the picture which the memory stored.

The exact 'present' in the strict sense never exists in our consciousness – the very second we reflect over the present it is already past. The present is always an unconscious experience. In the same way, the way of painting with water-colour about which I am talking here is rarely a conscious thing, but more an instinctive using of learned patterns.

In my water-colour painting, though, I am usually too impatient to prepare myself as carefully as the Zen Buddhist ideal imagines one should. So, small amendments are made. But I always strive to pick up all visual impressions, concentrate on the subject in that fleeting moment so that I almost do not sense the ground.

The water-colour has a very strong position, especially in British art tradition. Turner is an obvious starting point, but the technique generally is frequently found in English 19th-century painting. How do you relate to these traditions?

As both a water-colour painter and an ornithologist, one has, consciously or not, connections with the British tradition. For a water-colorist, the English landscape with its hazy air and changing skies is made for light wash work. On those occasions when I have had the opportunity to travel through England or south Scotland, as well as Ireland, it felt as if the landscape itself was a water-colour painting: the colour tones run into each other and the distant patches of woodland dissolve like patches applied to damp water-colour paper. Turner is an exceptional artist in his expressiveness and in his exuberant light. In his more thoroughly worked water-colours, which were the only ones which his contemporaries were allowed to witness, he does, however, use quite a dry brush and these are almost more reminiscent of tempera paintings. His preliminary studies, on the other hand, have a lightness and a flow which give a wonderful water-colour feel. For studying water-colour techniques, I also like to look at Thomas Girtin (1775–1802) and, perhaps even more so, John Singer Sargent (1856–1925).

In the British water-colour tradition I am strongly attracted to the tranquil and objectively observed quality, but I find the ambitiously 'pretty', as is manifested in some of the Victorian water-colours, more difficult. In the culture that has developed from the topographical painting there is an everyday realism, a sober observance and with economical expression, for which I feel more strongly, as for example in the works of John Sell Cotman (1782–1842) and, among wildlife-painters, Eric Ennion (1909–1980) and John Busby. They are important upholders of such a tradition of observation and economy of expression, an attitude based on a broad English empirical tradition – relying on one's own eyes – like Thomas Bewick and Gilbert White. When British painters become too 'emotional', the result is often artificial and overworked – sublime beauty is something which the Italians or French master better. A telling example is that of Charles F. Tunnicliffe (1900–1979), whose finished pieces are rather boring to my eyes. His studies of dead birds (usually called 'the measured drawings'), which he collected as reference material over a long lifetime, are in my view, and that of many others, the high point of his life's work. He did them for himself, looking at a dead bird directly in front of him, and without any thoughts of selling or showing. In his black-and-white woodcuts and field studies there is also a sense of restraint that gives them a feeling of conviction.

Like so many other artists, and Anders Zorn springs to my mind, you came late to oil-painting after having spent a long time improving your water-colour technique. Why do you think this is so? And in what way does oil-painting differ from water-colour painting or drawing?

When painting in oil, one carefully selects a hue and puts it down, all the time knowing that it can be removed or radically changed. In water-colour painting, the definite choice

must be made before the colour is applied on the paper. Sure, you can make corrections on a water-colour, for example by soaking up the colour with a sponge or a piece of tissue, if it is completely wrong, and it can also be mixed with other colours before it dries etc. But in reality these corrections are never an alternative at the moment one applies the colour, especially in certain sensitive stages involving large areas of water or sky. In this way the spontaneous water-colour is an expression of absolute concentration and presence, as in the ink washes described by Suzuki.

Oil has more of a 'conversational' quality, it has an inherent sluggishness. The colour is applied as a question, not as a statement. The colour in the brushstroke which I just applied asks if it is OK, if it is in tune with intentions and other brushstrokes. In this way a communication takes place between the painter and the canvas. The water-colour is a dialogue between the artist and the subject,

while the oil is a dialogue between the painting and the painter.

I feel that I have still not matured as a painter. I feel that there are still many conversations to be held between me and the canvas. But in the case of Zorn, and many others like him, it is probably more about the expression of the water-colour being created more by structure, form and drawing with the brush than is the case with the oil, which communicates more by colour. Perhaps a certain degree of maturity or experience of life is needed to be able to express oneself in colour?

In the following essay, you have described in greater detail what the work on one of your oil-paintings can be like: how different considerations and aesthetic choices lead to the final expression. It is a large painting showing a group of Pintails resting at a wetland. It is based on a series of sketches and water-colours done at different times and in different geographical locations.

Form och skugga [Shape and shadow], 2001
Eider
Water-colour 32x50 cm

127

Arctic Canada Geese
Hastings, Nebraska, 21 March 1984
Water-colour 36x48 cm

Main road, Rough-legged Buzzard
South Dakota, 22 March 1984
Pencil 13.5x21 cm

REST AFTER A LONG FLIGHT
PINTAILS

Some paintings are born while they are being painted, immediate visual impressions which pour down over a sheet of paper or are stroked onto a canvas. Others mature slowly in the head or develop from a simple sketch.

The painting shows some Pintails resting around a pool, perhaps meltwater on a spring meadow or the edge of a bog in a northern landscape. Their place is geographically undefined, but they still belong somewhere.

When Pintails arrive at my Gotland coast in late March they always appear in pairs, initially always far out in the bay. Not until April, when the females start searching for a nesting site, do they appear around the small pools on the coastal meadows. One grey morning in early April, following a cold night with wind and snow, I make my way across the littoral meadows to my studio. At one pool I am inspired by the snow melting on the grey-brown tufts of last year's sedge and grass: everything is so grey and yet full of subtle hues and pretty patterns, a beautiful background for a pair of Pintails. In the studio, I put down some basic colour combinations and the structure of the landscape on a larger canvas, and sketch a pair of Pintails on a sedge tussock.

As so often when I start without a thought-out plan or idea, the elements are out of tune and I had to make many changes along the way. Positioning or planting birds in an environment that is in itself a subject worth painting is difficult. Areas of vegetation and spatial formations to which I have taken a liking can become obscured, or the birds perhaps break up a line or a perspective that I would rather like to keep. The birds in themselves also place demands on where they can be positioned, as they are naturally attracted to certain spots in the imaginary landscape. So, it easily results in a kind of silent battle between the elemental parts, and something has to be given up. In this case, my instinctive feeling was that one single pair would be wrong.

At the same moment as I rejected the pair in favour of a group, I was mentally freed from the small wetland that had initially inspired me. A flock of Pintails would never occur there. My thoughts now left that pool, seeking references from somewhere else. I was in Japan in the previous winter and had sketched some Pintails in a wintry environment, where both snow and ochre-toned grass created the backdrop. They were already there among all the other sketches I had pulled out for this job. The Japanese sketches formed the basis for some of the birds' postures, but the place in question was seething with life, with cranes, people, Black Kites and various others. The painting for which I had just laid the foundations had a more desolate atmosphere, a certain feeling of remoteness. I felt myself as a lone observer.

An image that had in some way been suspended in the background then came to the fore, an image which I knew was preserved in one of my sketchbooks from spring 1984. An open, gently rolling landscape near Valentine, Nebraska, on the border with South Dakota, on 22nd March. Isolated farms, straight roads in a brown landscape with strands of grey-white snow. Stubble fields, dry slopes and rows of bushes along the streams that are sunk into small valleys, 'bottomlands'. After having watched some displaying Sharp-tailed Grouse since dawn, I drove around at random along the bypaths. The occasional Rough-legged Buzzard embellished the telegraph poles and sandy-coloured Horned Larks ran around in the gravel on the tracks, but I did not see any human beings. Then I came upon a group of Pintails and Teals on a flooded part of a field, at the edge of a field of oats which there was presumably never time to harvest. The sun had just penetrated through a faint morning mist, and the birds appeared very distinctive and

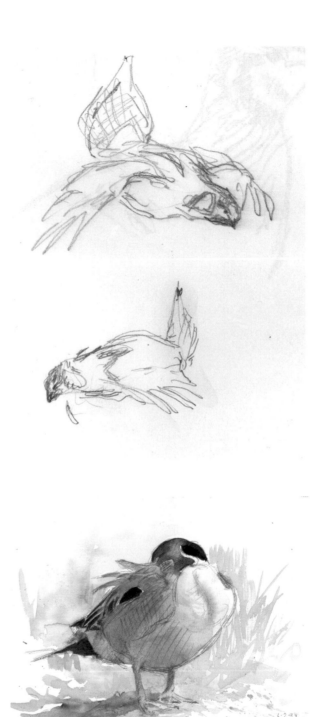

Study of displaying Sharp-tailed Grouse
Nebraska, 22 March 1984
Pencil 21x13.5 cm

Study of sleeping Pintail
Japan, 6 February 1999
Water-colour 25x32 cm

Sketchbook: Study of Pintail
Nebraska, 1984
Water-colour 33x41 cm

attractive and were very close. They were busily engaged in foraging and almost reluctant to take notice of me. A number of distinct characters etched themselves into my memory: The male's long, bluish-grey bill with a broad black band on top as if it were lacquered. The soft brown, nondescript colour of the head with a slight bronzy tone on the crown, discreet but refined thanks to the narrow white triangle on the nape. The small, rounded eye. The actually white underparts that tend to take on a colouring of yellow or ochre from the water, sometimes almost salmon-pink from humus-rich bog waters. The reflection of its colours in the water created an almost mystical sense of space. I managed to do a water-colour sketch before the Pintails took off to continue their journey northwards. I was so mesmerised by the spectacle that I remember saying to myself: I just have to paint this! But other spectacular sights intervened. Now, however, that stored experience of what I had witnessed in Nebraska emerged, as a sort of reference for atmosphere. These birds were admittedly active rather than passive, but there was something of the atmosphere in the surrounding landscape, something brooding.

When I am searching for a composition, a way of handling the shapes that arise or are contemplated as being part of a picture, the method is often one of trial and error. I feel my way forward, try out things, remove or change things until it is right. I do not really know whether I am guided by my own aesthetics or by certain prescribed mathematical laws, but I often think the latter. The composition is not the atmosphere, but it can either promote or counteract it. It is not unusual, therefore, for well-executed or successful parts in a painting to become meaningless if they are not supported by the composition; this can be a bird with its shadow, a tuft with snow on it, or a reflection in the water.

Living birds, if there are more than one, always have some kind of relationship to each other. They will always define a relationship among themselves and create a sense of spaciousness. When one uses five figures or more, a group is normally created where the presence of individuals is downplayed in favour of the collective. Two individuals must have an inter-relationship in order not to split the picture into two, and the same applies for the number four if it makes up two pairs. If you have four figures, however, three can be together while the fourth is free from the group. Five immediately provide more alternatives.

From the moment I started to place a number of birds in the painting, it obtained a life of its own, started to speak for itself on its own terms. The smaller group of six birds (fig 1) was increased to nine (fig 3) but finally became eight (fig 4). Since I was searching for a feeling of calm or, rather, a sense of waiting, the expres-sions on most of them were toned down. I made the male in the background retract his neck, and the one in the centre of the picture twist its head up vertically towards the plane of the picture (fig 3). They were made to become a collective unit. The females' greyish-brown and ochre tones naturally give them a more

introverted expression; in a way, they make up part of the vegetation structure. Whereas the males' facial expressions had to be restrained, the females' gentler faces could be allowed to be having a clear look at me without upsetting the whole.

I continued working on the background and the individual birds, but had difficulties in getting a feeling of space and depth in the picture. The female positioned diagonally in front of the male in the centre was moved about a number of times before she got her final posture, turning towards the group (fig 4). Her lines then led the eye towards the ducks in the background and gave the notion of a gateway leading into the place where the others were positioned. I then saw that the male in the middle was in fact the figure which made the extent of the spatial depth impossible. Because of his posture he marked the longitudinal direction that was also expressed by the background, which meant that he created what seemed like a glass wall between him and the ducks in the background. When I turned his head slightly towards me again (fig 5), this invisible wall was broken and he allowed me to enter the picture. The pair in the foreground now formed instead a flap-opening leading towards the birds and the habitats beyond. The rightmost female, her markings and her immediate surroundings became more interesting with this new perspective, and she was developed as a result of this.

The pair at rest at the far left in the picture was initially busy preening (figs 4, 5). A number of postures were tried out before the two acquired their final shape (fig 8). The most interesting thing that happens in their proximity, however, is the change to the background. At first, they are standing at the edge of the water on a vegetated snowy shore which continues beyond them (figs 1-6). When I painted a tongue of water extending in behind them (fig 7), the place on which the birds were standing appeared more like a

FIG 1.

FIG 2.

FIG 3.

FIG 4.

Various stages in the work on
Rest after a long flight

small spit of land. The male thereby came to be positioned on the rear 'shore' of this spit (fig 8). The whole area where the birds are resting now appeared as a small eminence partly sur-rounded by water, like a tiny peninsula. The place which the birds had chosen as a stop-over seemed all at once to be completely natural, they had found their way there themselves. The Pintails now had a place which was more obvious in the land-scape. This proved to be decisive, it created a perspective. The marshy ground behind the birds was lowered and appears flat until the ground rises again in a gentle slope in the background. The patches of snow in the background were remodulated to back up this perspective. The long, uniformly wide string of snow on the right side of the picture was removed (fig 6). It stopped the eye from moving up to the grassy slope. In the finished picture the strips of snow form a slight yet obvious eminence, a 'peak', in the background to the left of centre. A shallow triangle is created, which incorporates a large and a small oblong patch of snow. In addition, I painted a small tussock in the right-hand part of the picture (fig 6), obliquely above and behind the female standing farthest to the right. The tussock is the extension of the right side of the triangle.

During the spring I was often out in the field searching for Pintails on my local patch, the coastal meadows, to find fuel for the picture. The feeling of not, after all, properly understanding or totally mastering the males' markings and rhythmical structures and the females' patterns is very frustrating. When I worked on the faces of the various females, I felt a strong need for contact with live birds. One morning, in exceptionally fortunate circumstances, a female Pintail was standing alone on the very tussocks from which I had drawn my original inspiration (see page 121). Now spring had lured her ashore to seek a suitable site for egg-laying, but now she was surrounded by sprouting sedge and orchid buds.

The place where the Pintails had chosen to rest up was perhaps transferred more and more to a more Arctic environment as the Got-land spring progressed. I do not now know whether the ducks are caught on a chilly April morning on my coastal meadows, on a March day in Nebraska or on the Siberian tundra.

In the case of the Pintails, you describe how you try to find a composition, that the picture acquired a life of its own, began to talk on its own terms. It can be difficult to understand how this conversation sounds, for is it not the artist who dictates the appearance of the picture?

What I am trying to describe is that, in a painting, exciting dynamics often spring up between the different elements of the picture. If I turn the head of one bird, this affects the expression of the others. A bird that has been in a non-prominent position and had an insignificant facial expression can suddenly insist on 'saying' something, and I must then either define what it says or, alternatively, have it turn its head away or fall asleep. In this way, the picture can 'call upon' me to take it in a certain direction. At every moment I read the effect of a brushstroke, or a series of brushstrokes, how they change the picture and what the result invites me to do. Studio painting therefore becomes a kind of dialogue between me and the canvas. The picture thus stops referring to what I have seen – it refers only to what I see when I paint. It seeks its own goal through me. Therein lies the big differ-ence compared with painting in water-colour.

Paintings that I do in my studio are almost invariably based on an experience or a visual picture, usually documented in sketches or a water-colour. When I embark on them I am initially guided by a kind of inner vision. As the picture develops on the canvas, I see new possibilities or problems, and the vision changes during the course of the work. I usually draw my figures with a charcoal pencil until I find a composition. This phase often

becomes protracted and can be very frustrat-ing. It is important to feel from the begin-ning that the composition of a painting is structurally sound.

The painting 'Rest after a long flight' is carried out in the studio with a number of sketches as starting points. Most of your water-colours, on the other hand, are done outdoors with the subject before you. Are most oil-paintings done in the studio in the same way as 'Rest after a long flight'?

This varies. In recent years, I have painted oils as much in the field as in the studio. When I say in the field, it is usually from my car, a minibus. If the canvas is a large one, however, it becomes cramped, as the tele-scope also takes up some room. The car func-tions as a hide, which means that I cannot leave it or open the doors if the models are shy. But if weather and the subject allow, I prefer to sit outside. Gotland is very windy, though, and only very rarely is it calm enough for me to be able to sit out in the open with the canvas set up on the easel. The big disad-vantage with being ensconced inside the roomy yet restricted interior of the car is that it is hard to get a perspective on what I am painting.

With the subject directly in front of me, for example a group of Common Eiders on a rock, I have to work quickly in the knowledge that the scene is changeable. The combination of having to hurry and having a limited perspective means that I am often forced to make compromises in the composition. Instead of spending much time in getting correct proportions and postures with the charcoal pencil, I set to work as soon as I have sketched down something worth painting.

FIG 5.

FIG 6.

FIG 7.

FIG 8.

Vila efter en lång flykt [Rest after a long flight], 2000
Pintail
134   Oil   110x180 cm

This sometimes creates major deficiencies in the composition, which can be difficult to rectify at a later stage. A conflict often develops between changing the composition radically and the desire to retain certain parts that I am happy with. There is usually only one way out: change the composition or start a new canvas.

When I paint outdoors, any deficiencies in the composition are often compensated by the painting acquiring a specific light or colour scheme which cannot be repeated indoors.

Is there a big difference between painting in oils in the studio and outdoors? You mention light effects which you have committed to the canvas outdoors but which cannot be repeated in the studio. Is it not possible to create atmospheres and light in the studio, perhaps with the aid of oil or water-colour originals done in the field?

Of course they can, but the light becomes different. I do not put a negative value on this – the studio-created atmosphere can be at least as interesting. But it rarely has the naturalness which a painting done outdoors can have. When one paints outdoors, the painting is to a certain extent influenced by chance events in the same way as happens with the water-colour, but on another plane. The colour palette becomes different from when it is worked out in the studio. The combination of watching the subject in the telescope and at the same time sitting in a changing light opens up new ways of seeing things. Here there is scope for small fortuitous emendments which often become interesting. Some atmospheric conditions related to humidity, the amount of particles in the air, time of the day and so on create optical effects which the eye registers somewhat unconsciously. In the field I can work systematically with a shifted colour scale, dependent on, for example, a yellowish haze which I may not directly see. At home in the studio, I can then be surprised at how much of the atmosphere has crept in.

In the same way, one can be amazed by the effects of daylight if one has been painting under artificial light. When I started on 'Parad i Karahavet' (page 119) under fluorescent light, I had to 'retune' all the colour tones when I saw it in daylight the day after. Indoors it is easy for the colour treatment gradually to shift in accordance with one's expectations, for black to become black and white become white. It is impossible in practice to work out the colour scale of an object illuminated by an unnatural light. In the outdoor situation, I record these tinges of colour that make up the 'picture' of this light. For example, if I paint breaking waves and see that the white foam has a green hue, I may try adding some cobalt-green to the white. If that colour does not do the trick, I may stare intensely into the breakers again in order to find a new one. Chance occurrences perhaps cause me to suspect a red tone, so I add a little madder. Suddenly I see that the red and the green together, side by side and in different proportions in the white, create the light effect I have been looking for. In the studio, there is a tendency instead to look for a ready-mixed colour to solve a similar problem of tones.

It is mostly about looking, all the time recording with the eyes and tuning in with one's inner being.

It is my experience that rocks and boulders, with their varied colours of minerals and crystals, easily become 'dead' in the studio light. Outside I constantly encounter minor differences in shades which create light and air. Even the greyest of rocks have a play of light and a colour scale the entire essence of which is built up by subtle shades, maybe in the shape of lichens or algae at their base, or simply the reflection from an adjacent rock.

Many of the earlier landscape-painters, before the impressionists, worked on oil or water-colour sketches outdoors, working these up later in the studio. Almost without exception, the paintings lost the freshness that could be found in their sketches.

Schack [*Chess*], 1999
Grey Plover
Oil 110x180 cm

Painting at Aurriv
August 1999

136

Did they not see that? Maybe it was a conscious choice during the era of, say, romanticism. The fresh sky painted in the open air was perhaps too commonplace, not ideal enough. The clientele perhaps sought the 'unreal' atmosphere it dreamed of. Sometimes when I am in my studio and creating light, the result is often a little old-fashioned or traditional, to which my reaction is not always a negative one. I can imagine that it gives a sense of mystery. Created light is, of course, also a light.

In a text in the book Dagrar, *you have written a bit about the problems of finding the correct tints in oil-painting. In this case it was about the white parts of Magpies and the tones in snow (p. 19): 'Doing snow is like making a well-balanced sauce, one has to feel one's way ahead, get a balance between the tones. The white oil-paint – zinc, titanium or Chinese white – cannot be uniform, as it then becomes flat and lifeless. I am tempted, however, in this daylight: snow painted with pure zinc white and the shadows broken with only a touch of ivory black. When I paint in a continuum without the colour having time to dry, my brushes always have some ultramarine, English red or umber at the base of the bristles, so the white colour is rarely pure. I see how the subtle shades make snow materialise…'*

You have no formal training as a painter, you are self-taught, an autodidact. An integral part of your profession, nevertheless, is knowledge of, for example, solvents, preparation of canvas, watercolour techniques and paper qualities. How have you picked up the technical knowledge and the skills which you undeniably possess?

Mainly through working. By trying things out and experimenting. Certainly, it sometimes strikes me that I have perhaps used much mental effort in an attempt to understand the materials, something that would maybe have been considerably easier to assimilate through books or a teacher. My interest in the purely technical details, in

Frisk vind [Fresh wind], 2001
Oil 80x120 cm

other words accessories in the form of solvents, emulsions, canvas-primers etc., has, however, been exceedingly small. I cannot deny that I am fascinated by the idea, from a romantic starting point, of doing everything from the very basics, but have never found the calmness to do it. My inclination has always been towards the creative process in itself, seeing things happen. Instruction manuals often bore me to tears – I want to get started and see results.

My attempts at trying to understand and master the techniques which I see in such old masters as Velasquez or Zorn have in many respects come about through watching rather than reading. Over the years, however, an interest in the people behind the works, and with that also the literature about them, has come to fascinate me. For a painter, there is nothing more useful than to stand in front of

an original and just study it. To copy a work is perhaps even better, but I have never done this. It seems unexciting to me.

In connection with your field guides, we have talked about the photograph as a reference. The use of photographs as a starting point is also widespread within wildlife-painting. To what degree do you use photographs when you paint pictures other than those to be used for field identification?

The American bird-painter Don Eckelberry – outspoken and with a sharp pen – coined the expression 'the Kodachrome school'. The simple replication in paint of a photograph is always a complete failure. There are many wildlife-painters who regularly start from a photograph. Some paintings are so photographically exact that all the optical phenomena which characterise the photograph can

137

Life study, 1981
Water-colour
57x39 cm

the artist's eye or mind left. If, for want of something to tell, one borrows the expression of the photograph, then the photograph of course becomes more interesting than the painted image.

Optical distortion has, through camera obscura and other techniques, influenced our perception of reality, and especially the artist's way of looking at optical effects of light, ever since the Renaissance. The photograph is the very basis for the impressionists' decoding of certain mobile elements in nature, such as water. This is nothing new, and I myself see my subjects through an eyepiece which, to some extent, produces the same displacement of perspectives as does a photograph taken through a telephoto lens. But almost all of my water-colours and most oils are painted outdoors straight from the subject, without the aid of the photograph. When working on a larger oil, however, I may often, for certain details, have recourse to a photo that I have taken.

In rare cases, the photograph can give birth to an idea for a picture. Maybe I happen to have taken a photo which has something special in the atmosphere that inspires me. The final result, however, never falls within the limited scope of the photograph.

What are your feelings with regard to details? While field guides and scientific illustration place high demands on details, these are hardly necessary for conveying impressions and atmospheres in nature. Much of wildlife-painting is, despite this, imprinted with details.

Some scientific illustration, as well as certain styles in painting, is characterised by an almost obtrusive sharpness in detail which can sometimes seem unreal. But it can also, when at its best, at almost magical, like a well-executed *trompe l'oeil* which erases the border between illusion and reality. It is not unusual for artists portraying animals and nature to endeavour to depict as many details

as possible – every hair in the fur, grain in the bark, every little pebble or pine needle on the ground. This passion for details, however, easily becomes an end in itself and can go beyond the stage of the illusory and instead become artificial. I can end up there myself sometimes, and then I want to take a step back, erase and paint over it in order to find the balance again. I also know how easy it is for want of a successful composition or shape to use 'make-up' on the picture or to decorate it with details to conceal its shortcomings. Details that underline an integrated pictorial concept can be impressive, but in pictures which lack composition and depth they easily become high-faluting.

If one looks at your total production over the last 30 years, it is the birds that predominate. Other motifs, landscapes, mammals or humans, seem to be more occasional diversions. Do you feel that there are other subject areas that have a similar appeal to that of birds?

Many other themes attract me, and sometimes I fancy concentrating more on other motifs. Inspiration is not lacking. But I also have regard for the work that is necessary to penetrate a subject area. By that I do not mean just to do a good painting of, for instance, a mammal or a house interior. It is about getting so close to a subject area that I think that I can say something interesting about it in the painting. Landscapes are probably what are closest to me, and they are also close to my birds. When I am outdoors, it is just as much the landscape and the sky that inspire me to paint. In the end, it is nevertheless usually the birds that have to express the landscape. Large mammals also appeal to me.

Primarily, however, I have felt a desire to paint portraits of people. In certain respects this is not so far removed from the bird portrait – it is about observing and understanding the subject. I have regularly done occasional portraits over the years, and I

be seen in them. They can in a way be said to be the wildlife-painting equivalent of the Chuck Close portraits of the early 1970s. Ultra-realism or photo-realism also gave artists using animals as subjects a legitimate reason to make every use of photos at that time. Unlike the ultra-realists, who make a point of their work being photographic, these artists saw the photograph as a means of achieving truthfulness to life. Such photo-realistic paintings of wildlife, however, are to me more reminiscent of photography than of nature. Pictures that try to imitate a photograph, with the aim of being as close to real life as possible, risk becoming meaningless through the very fact that they renounce the presence of the artist. Using the photograph in order to understand a pattern or a detail is one thing, but when one copies entire arrangements and pictorial solutions there is little of always find it an exciting challenge. When I visit museums I frequently look at portraits, because they often say as much about the artist as about the person portrayed. In the same way as with birds, there is no substitute for having the subject directly in front of one – portraits painted from photographs are virtually always dull and uninteresting, except for some of Warhol's early iconographic portraits. It is an all but a mystery that this should be so.

Which other painters who use oil as a medium are you inspired by? I know that Bruno Liljefors is one of your most important paragons, but there must be other painters who have come to influence you in your work?

Bruno Liljefors (1860–1939) has had a dominant influence not only on Swedish wildlife-painting, but also on the Swedes' way of looking at their wildlife. He has been of major significance in my own development so far as oil-painting is concerned. As a youngster, I regarded Liljefors as old-fashioned and gloomy. In a diary entry from Gotland on 31st December 1968, at the sight of a beautiful winter landscape, I state: 'One gets the desire to start painting with oils. One thinks of Bruno Liljefors's pictures at dusk from the winter archipelago'.

Liljefors was hardly in the archipelago in the wintertime, so I must have had quite a diffuse perception of his paintings when I was a fifteen-year-old. Since the 1970s, however, I have consciously studied Liljefors and learned from him. From the start I was simply amazed and awestruck by his genius. I tried to paint as well as he. Then I tried to avoid him, feeling that he was somehow in the way. I felt obliged to find his errors and shortcomings, commit a secret act of patricide. The relationship matured. I now see him as a person who is very close to me. I can appreciate his unique qualities and at the same time see his human characteristics, that his shortcomings, too, are part of the person one likes.

Another painter whom I have studied and who has had an influence on my own development is Anders Zorn (1860–1920). His technique in both oil and water-colours leaves me speechless with admiration. If there is any reason to talk about illusionist painting in the sense of magic, then Zorn is a good example of this. I have also been inspired by several Russian painters, for example Ilya Repin (1844–1930), Abram Arkhipov (1862–1930) and Isac Levitan (1860–1900). It is not only their divine way of painting but also their strong ties to the Russian landscape, to the countryside and its culture, that impresses me. Levitan, as a landscape-painter, has done several paintings over which I can sit and contemplate for a long time. There are many other artists.

I can feel a strong primitive attraction towards painting, towards creating a feeling of truth. Maybe it is faithfulness to nature that I am seeking. The feeling of clear vision, the order of things, a 'this-is-the-way-it-is' feeling. The inspiration is nature: it is therein that I look for an answer. To what I do not know, but through painting nature I feel that I come closer to the answer. I come back to the word 'self-evident'. Maybe a similar feeling as a religious revelation could be that at a certain moment one thinks that one sees 'the truth'. Whether this is a goal to aim for or not is something on which I really have no opinion, but the feeling is just there in me. Science, philosophy, art and religion are all different ways in which to get closer to the truth.

I look for it in the play of light around an Avocet in shallow water, in the reflection of the sky among the rocks, in the haze hanging over dry grassland, by trying to unravel a Woodcock from its pattern or to search for the right facial expression on a Wheatear. Why there exactly?

Because I imagine that it is there – my truth.

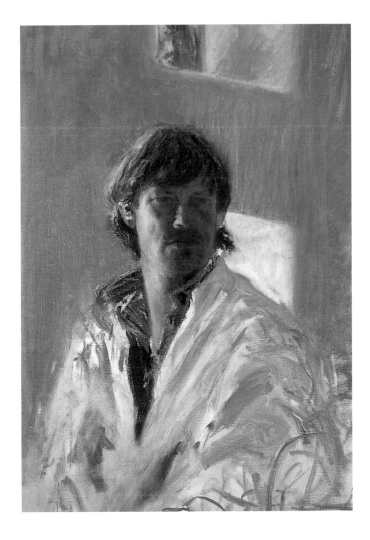

Self-portrait (detail), 1994
Oil 160x140 cm

139

I think that you have, in a passage in the book Dagrar, *probably summed up well what you are seeking in your relationship with nature, the birds, and in your painting. There, under the heading 'Thoughts towards late summer', you write about early memories, about how you have always painted birds and how you try to tell of the uniqueness in each encounter with a bird. You state there that nobody will ever see what you have seen. Perhaps this is true, but through your pictures and your words you let us see more than we would otherwise have seen.*

Man likes to seek explanations for his actions, looks in the register of interpretative models and established values. But explanations rarely satisfy the sense of feeling, they just dress it in words, but the emotive influence, the abstract element that drives one onwards, never has a name.

I have watched birds, described, painted and drawn them, studied and researched their lives and habits for so long that the reason for my actions, the driving force itself, has perhaps changed. Maybe it is a state of mind from early years that has deepened, altered and developed to become the simple nest of a bird in the cup of which I become real. When the sight of a Wood Sandpiper's light steps over the mud or the Black-headed Gull's pursuit of caddis-flies across the evening sky overwhelms me with a sense of tranquillity, I ponder over this. Maybe I have, by changing interests and goals, constructed a womb – to which I can return, alone, with myself – fully satisfied by watching, just observing and feeling enclosed by what is the obvious, the self-evident. I ask questions. What is it that the Jackdaws are taking when they bounce down from the fence posts? How does the sun make a pattern on the translucent wing of a juvenile Common Gull? Where did the Whimbrels that passed by a

moment ago come down to rest? Questions which in reality do not need an answer, but are more the stirring of a thought when the eye sees.

But, as so often happens, the light gathers, becomes condensed from some atmospheric stress in the east, reaches my wavelength. It is as if the light finds its way into my inner being, my soul, my sensory cycle, and is demanding some action, an impulse to use this light/impression for a specific goal such as a sketch or painting.

A Swallow lands for a split second on the sand – somewhat loose-winged, pale in its rusty bib, I see just a droplet in infinity and suddenly I want to capture, document, seek answers. Maybe the visit lasts for a minute, the young Swallows dance above the sandflies' broad atlas, 'slivitt' they call and are suddenly off, heading southwest over the fields of turning thistles. I had something to relate which I think is important, but I never managed really to see what – oh yes, I saw, I saw but … only I and no-one else. Nobody else will ever see what I have seen.

Faludden
3rd October 2000
Water-colour 42x56 cm

Disig sömn [*Hazy Sleep*]
Aurriv 17 april 2001
Skärfläcka
142   Akvarell 32×50 cm

Småspov invid sten [*Whimbrel beside rock*]
May 1996
Water-colour 36x51 cm

143

Study of drake Eider, 2001
Water-colour 25x32 cm

144

Female Eider
Rivet, 16 August 2000
Water-colour 42x56 cm

145

Great Black-backed Gulls, 1993
Water-colour 58x75 cm

31.10.01 Sndre

Juvenile Herring Gull
31 October 2001
Water-colour 32x50 cm

147

Aurriv, 07.30 hours on 4 October 2001
Golden Plover
148   Water-colour 36x51 cm

Thi Giuseppina
Avon 0750 4.10.01

Stuckvike
20 April 2002
150   Water-colour 38x57 cm

Rummet hos en ung Kustsnäppa [*Room for a juvenile Knot*]
Aurriv, 30 September 2000
Water-colour 42×56 cm

151

Kvällsvandraren [*The evening wanderer*], 1987
Woodcock

152   Water-colour 45x68 cm

Grå vinterjägare [*Grey winter hunter*]
13 February 1987
Sparrowhawk
Water-colour 42x56 cm

Golden Eagle
Hoburgen, 3 October 2000
156   Water-colour 42x56 cm

Field hare, 2000
Water-colour 36x51 cm

Woodcock with young, 1987
Water-colour 45x68 cm

Tree Sparrow
Sindarve, 18 January 1991
160   Water-colour 25x32 cm

Rödhakar överallt [*Robins everywhere*]
Faludden, 14 October 2000
Water-colour 42x56 cm

161

View from studio
February 1994

162 Water-colour 75x104 cm

Blackbird pair, 1991
Water-colour 44x67 cm

Raven 1993
Water-colour
51×36 cm

165

Study for *Bergets öga*
Water-colour 23.5x30 cm

Bergets öga [*The eye of the mountain*], 1986
Gyr Falcon
166   Water-colour 80x120 cm

Raven study, 1994
168   Water-colour 44×67 cm

Karaktärer [*Characters*]
31 October 2001
Rooks
Water-colour 40x55 cm

169

Troget par [*Faithful couple*]
Extremadura, 9 February 1994
Griffon Vultures
Water-colour 31x41 cm

Tidig vårmorgon [*Early spring morning*], 1983
Short-eared Owl
Oil 100x105 cm

Arktiskt möte [*Arctic encounter*], 1985
Spectacled Eider
Oil 83x123 cm

173

Arktiska mönster [*Arctic patterns*], 1993
Gyr Falcon
174   Oil 78x115 cm

176   Shoveler pair, 2001
           Oil 80x120 cm

På vakt [*On guard*], 2001
White-fronted Goose
Oil 80x120 cm

Potatisätarna [*The potato-eaters*], 1993
Rooks
178   Oil 110x180 cm

Samstämda [*In accord*], 1992
Waxwing
180   Oil 76x60 cm

Oktober, 1998
Blackbird
Oil 61x46 cm   181

Min fågel [*My bird*], 1999
Bullfinch
182   Oil 46x61 cm

Vinterfölje [*Winter covey*], 1999
Grey Partridge
Oil 110x180 cm

Nyanlända [*Newly arrived*], 1998
Curlew
Oil 80x120 cm

Ensam på toppen
[*Alone on the peak*], 1997
Gyr Falcon
Oil 81x100 cm

Natt vid Kolyma [*Night on the Kolyma*], 1992
White-billed Diver
188   Oil 140x200 cm

Common Gull and rocks, 1987
Oil 72x92 cm

Sidor av ljus [Aspects of light], 1987
Avocet
Oil 90x120 cm

Passage, 2001
Avocet
Oil 73x100 cm

Den vita färgen [The colour white], 2001
Avocet
Oil 46x61 cm

198

Tre unga spovar [*Three young godwits*], 2000–01
Bar-tailed Godwit
Oil 81x120 cm

Grått skimmer [*Grey glow*], 1998
Caspian Tern
Oil 83x92 cm

Mot alla vindar [*Against all winds*], 2001
Great Black-backed Gull
Oil 81x100 cm

Åtrå [*Desire*], 1998–99
Eider
204   Oil 110x180 cm

I dyningarna [*In the swelling waves*], 2000
Eider
Oil 61x80 cm

En stund på stenen [*A moment on the rock*], 2001
Eider
Oil 80x120 cm

Ögat [*The eye*], 2000
Grey Plover
208   Oil 38x46 cm

I printed my first lithograph in 1977, and up to and including May 2002 I have printed 77 different sheets. The method which I use is based on painting or drawing on a coarse plastic film. This is a thick sheet of plastic which is sandpapered to correspond to the surface possessed by polished limestone. On this surface I am able to draw in pencil and apply a wash of black gouache or Indian ink. The drawing is then transferred on to an aluminium plate, from which the subject is printed.

I rarely work with an exact original but allow the subject to develop during the course of the printing, starting from one or more water-colour sketches. For each individual colour which is to be printed, a new separate plastic sheet is painted with just black colour or pen. The saturation of the black gouache on the film determines the saturation of the printed colour. On the metal plate I can scrape or grind down surfaces which are too compact or remove altogether parts which I do not want. The picture is gradually built up by adding one colour after another. The number of colours is usually about 15. In some cases I leave a broad white frame around the picture, but in most cases I tear off the edges of the printed sheet so that the finished picture bleeds off to a ragged edge.

The printing work has taken place in Stockholm in close collaboration with a printer. In the early years I worked with Arne Andersson and in later years with John Åkerlund at Järla Grafik.

The printed sheets are signed at the bottom in the right-hand corner and numbered on the left in Arabic figures. The HC edition is numbered in Arabic or Roman figures; HC is an abbreviation for 'hors de commerce', which means 'not for general sale'.

In the mid-1970s I also signed and numbered six different reproductions printed in offset. The first of these, 'Juvenile Common Gull', was printed in black-and-white and issued in a folder in 1975 (260 copies). A four-sheet portfolio entitled 'Winter birds' was issued in 1976 (200 copies). The sixth, 'Sparrowhawk with Bullfinch prey', was published by WWF Sweden in a folder in 1976 (350 copies).

During the 1980s, Mill Pond Press in Florida published seven of my originals (four oils, two gouaches and one water-colour) in the form of signed and numbered art prints in an edition of 950 copies. I discontinued this issue in 1987.

1

2

3

4

5

6

7

8

1. Chaffinches in winter birch
   57x43 cm 1977
   Limited edition 1–215/215
   HC I–XX/XX

2. Whooper Swans in sea bay
   45x61 cm 1978
   Limited edn 1–350/350
   HC I–XXXV/XXXV

3. Lapwing on March field
   45x62 cm 1978
   Limited edn 1–350/350
   HC I–XXXV/XXXV

ÖN, 1983
Portfolio of 4 lithographs
Limited edn 1–250/250
HC 1–25/25

4. Beside grass-leaved orache.
   White Wagtail
   63x48 cm

5. Avocet keeping its young
   warm
   48x63 cm

6. Pintails at dusk
   48x63 cm

7. Arctic Terns on sand
   48x63 cm

8. Arctic Tern's nest
   25x48 cm 1983
   Limited edn 1–300/300
   HC 1–30/30

9 10 11

12 13 14 15 16

9. Caspian Tern
   34 _ 26 cm 1983
   Limited edn 1–200/200
   HC I–XX/XX
   Included with collector's
   edition of *Ön*

10. Summer Black-headed Gulls
    48x63 cm 1984
    Limited edn 1–100/100
    HC 1–10/10
    An edition on yellower
    paper I–L/L issued for the
    collector's edition in
    Norway of the book *Ön*
    (Öya)

11. Arctic Skua in rain haze
    48x63 cm 1984
    Limited edn 1–100/100
    HC 1–10/10
    I–L/L as above

American sketches, 1984
Portfolio of 5 lithographs
Limited edn 1–300/300

12. Arctic Canada Geese
    24 x30 cm

13. Bald Eagle
    30x24 cm

14. Northern Pygmy Owl
    30 x24 cm

15. Snowy Owl
    24x30 cm

16. Dark-eyed Juncos
    24 x 30 cm

17. Little Tern juvenile
    39x 57 cm 1986
    Limited edn 1–220/220
    HC 1–22/22

18. October gold. Goldfinch
    62x48 cm 1986
    Limited edn 1–250/250,
    HC 1–25/25

17 18

19

20

21

22

23

24

25

19. Heading south. Brent Goose
    64x91 cm 1986
    Limited edn 1–150/150
    HC 1–15/15

20. Sandwich Terns
    43x63 cm 1986
    Limited edn 1–175/175
    HC 1–17/17

21. Resting Avocets
    33x44 cm 1987
    Limited edn 1–100/100
    HC 1–10/10

22. Montagu's Harrier female
    38x30 cm 1987
    Limited edn 1–100/100
    HC 1–10/10

23. Sea Otter
    29x38 cm 1987
    Limited edn 1–120/120
    HC 1–15/15

24. Youthful charm. Curlew
    42x29 cm 1987
    Limited edn 1–100/100
    HC 1–10/10

25. Pairing. Avocet
    60x88 cm 1988
    Limited edn 1–200/200
    HC 1–25/25

26

27

26. The wagtail. White Wagtail
    64x46 cm 1988
    Limited edn 1–250/250
    HC 1–25/25

27. Winter vigil. Goshawk
    62x88 cm 1989
    Limited edn 1–250/250
    HC 1–25/25

28. Rough-legged Buzzard
    37x46 cm 1989
    Limited edn 1–80/80

29. Going to rest. Eider
    63x 83 cm 1990
    Limited edn 1–250/250
    HC 1–25/25

30. Garden Warbler and cherry blossom
    34 x27 cm 1990
    Limited edn 1–200/200
    HC 1–20/20
    Included with the collector's edition
    of *En dag i maj*

28

29

30

214

31

32

33

34

35

36

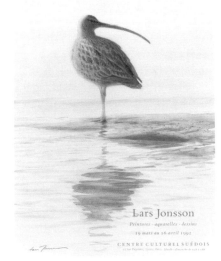

37

38

39

38. Signs of spring. Chaffinch
34x45 cm 1993
Limited edn 1–310/310
HC 1–30/30

39. On the eve of the journey.
Arctic Tern
64x81 cm 1993
Limited edn 1–310/310
HC 1–30/30

40. November apples. Magpie
50x70 cm 1993
Limited edn 1–310/310
HC 1–30/30

41. Under protection.
Caspian Tern
37x51 cm 1994
Limited edn 1–310/310
HC I–XXX/XXX
Issued by the postal authorities

42. The Raven
84x64 cm 1994
Limited edn 1–150/150

43. Shelducks
59x86 cm 1994
Limited edn 1–250/250
HC 1–25/25

40

41

42

43

44

45

46

47

48

49

44. One's own reflection. Wigeon
    47x64 cm 1994
    Limited edn 1–310/310
    HC 1–30/30

45. In autumn plumage. Redstart
    61x47 cm 1994
    Limited edn 1–310/310
    HC 1–30/30

46. Where the light is broken.
    Common Gull
    54x83 cm 1995
    Limited edn 1–310/310
    HC 1–30/30

47. The guardian. Jay
    51x68 cm 1995
    Limited edn 1–310/310
    HC 1–30/30

48. Encounter in the Kara Sea.
    Polar bear
    55x81 cm 1995
    Limited edn 1–310/310
    HC 1–30/30

49. Common Gull portrait
    20x27 cm 1996
    Limited edn 1–200/200
    HC 1–30/30

50. Pied Flycatcher
    26x24 cm 1996
    Limited edn 1–200/200
    HC 1–15/15

51. Collared Flycatcher
    44x37 cm 1996
    Limited edn 1–200/200
    HC 1–20/20

52. The right place. White Wagtail
    31x46 cm 1997
    Limited edn 1–310/310
    HC 1–30/30

53. Whimbrels at stopover
    36x57 cm 1998
    Limited edn 1–310/310
    HC 1–30/30

54. Among almond blossom. Lapwing
    32x44 cm 1997
    Limited edn 1–310/310
    HC 1–30/30

55. In the early evening. Avocet
    59x48 cm 1998
    Limited edn 1–310/310
    HC 1–30/30

56. Stranded beings. Wigeon
    60x87 cm 1997
    Limited edn 1–310/310
    HC 1–30/30

50   51   52

53   54

55   56

57

58   59

60

61   62

63   64   65

66   67   68

DAGRAR, 2000
Portfolio of 12 lithographs issued in
a case together with the book *Dagrar*,
half-bound
Limited edn 1–366/366
HC 1–40/40

57. The light. Magpie
     27x36 cm

58. Winter sketch. Great Tit
     36x27 cm

59. Back. Curlew
     27x36 cm

60. Shapes. Eider
     27x36 cm

61. Instant moment. Pied Flycatcher
     36x27 cm

62. Close. Ringed Plover
     27x36 cm

63. Summer night. Avocet
     36x27 cm

64. Nervous. Swallow
     27x36 cm

65. Autumn's colour. Robin
     36x27 cm

66. Sea swell. Herring Gull
     27x36 cm

67. Lookout. Peregrine Falcon
     36x27 cm

68. My bird. Bullfinch
     27x36 cm

69

69. Figures. Black-throated Diver
    42x59 cm 2000
    Limited edn 1–310/310
    HC 1–30/30

70. Daylights. Redshank
    41x59 cm 2000
    Limited edn 1–310/310
    HC 1–30/30

71. After the summer. Knot
    49x64 cm 2001
    Limited edn 1–310/310
    HC 1–30/30

72. Eclogue. Ruff
    40x55 cm 2001
    Limited edn 1–360/360
    HC 1–35/35

73. Rest. Avocet
    41x59 cm 2002
    Limited edn 1–310/310
    HC 1–30/30

70

71

72

27/150   [signature]

73

The studio in Hamra

Lars Jonsson was born on 22nd October 1952, in Stockholm. His father, Sven Jonsson, born in 1913, and his mother, May, née Gustavsson in 1926, had had the family's first child, Anders, thirteen months earlier. The third in the family of brothers and sisters, Eva, was born in 1956. Lars also had a half-sister, Helene, from his father's previous marriage.

From 1951 until the beginning of the 1970s the family lived in Farsta, a typical suburb of Stockholm. Here, on the border between town and country, with the city's main centre within commuting distance and with nature close at hand, he grew up. During the early days of his childhood, the country-side around this suburb, with its mixture of cornfields, woodland, meadows and ditches and its variety of bird species, came to be the subject of frequent visits, which he made alone or with his brother Anders. When, as a teenager, he started to keep a diary, it is bristling with notes on local outings and observations made in the countryside south of Stockholm, especially around Ågestasjön, a bird-rich reedy lake surrounded by forest and cultivated land. In the 1970s the family moved in stages to Gotland. In 1975 Lars took up residence in central Stockholm, and in the same year he acquired a large lime-stone house in southern Gotland.

Lars revealed his interest in birds at a very young age. A brown sheet of paper from March 1957 shows about ten patiently drawn birds, with tails, wings and bills. A pastel drawing from November 1957, when he had just reached the age of seven, illustrates a Green Woodpecker with all salient features. Also preserved are long tales and reports recorded in sequence on rolls of paper or in drawing-books. For Lars, as for so many other children, drawing and sketching and reporting were – obviously – a pleasurable

game, in which not least the saturated colours of the pastel crayons opened up a rich world of colour and shape. Birds are a constantly recurring theme. He tells of how he often climbed into trees and played at being a bird.

From the second half of the 1950s the family spent a few weeks' holiday every year on Gotland, an island in the Baltic Sea with an altogether singular wildlife. Here he came in contact with coastal meadows and bays richly populated with totally different bird species from those which he had encountered in the countryside around Farsta: ducks, waders, gulls and many others. The childlike curiosity over animals and nature was reinforced by reading the children's stories on animals, which were popular at that time. These books had a strong tendency to anthropomorphise animals, which gave a young reader ample opportunity to identify with the individual animal.

Lars Jonsson's interest in nature and birds deepened during his teenage years, and in 1967 he joined Fältbiologerna – the field biologists – a youth section of Svenska Naturskyddsföreningen [the Swedish Society for the Protection of Nature]. His skills in drawing and observing were sharpened, and his pictures attracted increasingly more attention. In autumn 1967, his talent was discovered by a curator at Sweden's Naturhistoriska Riksmuseet [the Natural History Museum], in Stockholm, when Lars was in the process of drawing birds in the museum's display cabinets. This resulted in his first exhibition, in 1968.

In Sweden there is a deep-rooted interest in nature from the days of Rudbeck and Linnaeus, and from the end of the 1800s a strong national tradition within wildlife-painting was established with Bruno Liljefors. When Lars Jonsson, as a fifteen-year-old, takes his first steps on the paths of this

Lars with his parents on the beach, Gotland, 1960

tradition, its contemporary upholders are primarily the artists Harald Wiberg and Gunnar Brusewitz but also Allan Andersson. They came to influence his art, and not only as role models but also as helpful and suppor-tive older fellow-artists. Slowly Lars Jonsson develops his own identity, an identity which is polarised in the more or less scientific study of nature and bird life with comrades in Fältbiologerna and an exploration – encouraged by many – of the individual's own role in a strong Swedish art tradition of nature portrayal. Knowledge and art.

Besides the brush and the water-colour paints, his tool becomes the telescope, with which he gets really close to the birds in a new way and gains fresh knowledge of their appearance.

Lars Jonsson's indisputable gift for capturing the character of birds and his deep ornithological knowledge mean that, when still only twenty, he is commissioned to formulate a new European field guide. The publishers' idea is that the book will consist of several parts, with each part devoted to one habitat. With great eagerness he gets stuck into the job, which from start to finish was to occupy his time throughout the 1970s, and which was to fill up his working days

223

again during much of the 1980s when he carries out a fundamental revision of the older edition. The field guide first appeared in five parts, the last being published in 1980, and from the outset was published in seven countries. This publication led to Lars Jonsson being regarded as one of the world's foremost bird-painters and also a leading authority on birds.

He himself describes the work on the field guide as his 'academy'. Interminable hours are devoted to putting together and painting the plates within strict frameworks, and in the process he refines his water-colour technique. On journeys around Europe and the Mediterranean countries, where he makes careful detailed studies of species and forms, his capacity for looking and recording develops. In the early 1970s he has already made contact with the international ornithological world, not least in England. His pictures appear in international journals, and include a water-colour on the front cover of *Birds*, the RSPB (Royal Society for the Protection of Birds) magazine, in 1973. His travels bring him into personal contact with authorities in his field, Robert Gillmor, Eric Ennion and, especially, the legendary field-guide author Roger Tory Peterson.

While the 1970s were to a large extent taken up by the field guide, an important event happens in his private life: in spring 1976 he moves into his own house near the southern tip of Gotland. And from that time onwards this house and the surrounding countryside become his permanent residence and focal point. He still lives alone, with his dog Columbus. His time is divided between work-related travel and writing and painting. Even though the artist takes a back seat to some extent during this period, he is all the time working with greater or lesser intensity on a series of water-colours and oils. He takes part in a number of exhibitions, among them the fundamentally important 'Animals in Art' at the Royal Ontario Museum in Canada in

1975. His first really big one-man exhibition after the one at Stockholm's Natural History Museum takes place in Gotland in 1979, arranged by Gotland's Konstförening [Gotland Art Society]. His reputation as an artist grows, even if still within limited circles.

In 1979 the first period of the field-guide work was over. He is soon to reach the age of thirty, and the early 1980s are characterised by a certain searching, not least in the artistic field. The many years of disciplined work on the field guide seem to have set off a desire to experiment. Travelling, now also to more remote places, becomes an important part of his life. Several significant periods of time are spent during these years in Spain in 1980, in Peru in winter 1981/82, and in USA in spring 1984 efter having first visited the country in autumn 1981, and he also makes a trip to Siberia in 1983. The year 1983 is a momentous one. He publishes the book *Ön*, a documentation in words and pictures of life on a small shoal of sand near his house in Gotland. The book is met with rapturous reviews, with attention being drawn not least to the sense of presence in Lars Jonsson's prose. He has a big exhibition at Naturhistoriska Riksmuseet, with pictures done in the 1970s and several large works from trips made in recent years. Also shown here is a 4-metre-wide canvas, which heralds a new dimension in his painting. In the same year he is soon to have three children, Martin (1985), Viktor (1987) and Rebecka (1988), and in 1994 Matilda was also born. With the house in Gotland, marriage and the children, a certain regularity enters into his life. The big single-volume version of the field guide is now finished. A one-man exhibition at The Tryon Gallery in London in 1987 is significant, bringing him a success which comes in the same year as his father dies.

Important phases in the mid-1980s are his communications with wildlife and artists in the USA. A long-held dream becomes a reality in 1984 when he is given the

Tambopata river, Peru, January 1982

224

opportunity for a period of several months to migrate with the birds in America, from Florida in the southeast to Alaska in the far northwest. From the shore of the Bering Strait he is able to see the Sandhill Cranes migrate across to Siberia, the place which he longs to visit more than any other. At this time he also makes contact with a number of prominent figures in American wildlife-painting, such as Don R. Eckelberry, Arthur Singer, Robert Verity Clem and the Canadian wildlife artist Robert Bateman. Also important is the meeting and friendship with the Swedish sculptor Kent Ullberg, who has been working in the USA since the mid-1970s.

Lars Jonsson's pictures are held in high regard, and he begins a successful collaboration with The Mill Pond Press and its influential publisher Robert Lewin, who publishes limited-edition prints of art. This association is broken off after a couple of years, since Lars feels that, as an artist, he cannot really develop within the limits of the American ideas of what a wildlife picture should look like. From 1982 he participates in an annual exhibition, 'Birds in Art', at the Leigh Yawkey Woodson Art Museum in Wisconsin, USA, where, in 1988, the honour of Master Wildlife Artist is conferred upon him, the youngest person hitherto to be awarded the distinction at that museum.

While travelling in North America he became intensely absorbed in the study of certain small waders of the genus *Calidris*, studies which resulted in papers being published in 1984 in the journals *American Birds* and *British Birds*. The idea of rewriting the field guides grows increasingly stronger, however, during the 1980s. Work on the revision implies a reworking of a large number of plates, an updating of research and new trips and field studies. But the great demand, and a personal feeling that the books should be amalgamated into one volume arranged according to a systematic grouping, mean that again he plunges

straight in to the exacting work that such an amalgamation involves. The work is arduous, and the artist side of him must once more step into the background. A follow-up to the book *Ön* nevertheless springs up in spring and summer 1989 as a result of an occasional change of work. It comes out in spring 1990 under the title *En dag i maj* [A day in May], and is an attempt to depict a single day, 18th May, in southern Gotland, from early morning to late evening.

In 1991 the new single-volume edition of the field guide, *Fåglar i Europa med Nordafrika och Mellanöstern*, is finished and, relieved, he is able to oversee the printing of the English edition, *Birds of Europe with North Africa and the Middle East*, which appears first. The Swedish edition followed in the next year. The book has appeared in a total of 13 languages and become a great commercial success. Relieved at having completed his great work, he realises a long-standing dream to go to the Siberian Arctic, in June 1991. The dream of the Siberian tundra Lars has carried with him since he was young, and he undertakes several journeys and expeditions there during the 1990s, in summer 1994 in the capacity as artist on the Swedish–Russian expedition 'Tundra ecology 94' – a scientific ship-based expedition which travelled in A. E. Nordenskiöld's footsteps along the Northeast Passage. In arctic Siberia he has the opportunity to study and draw many arctic bird species, as well as arctic foxes and polar bears. For the first time he has the chance to observe many arctic waders on their breeding grounds, birds which pass by his Gotland coast over a few short days in spring and autumn. The experiences from this trip are presented in an exhibition at the Naturhistoriska Riksmuseet in 1995, together with the work of two other artists who took part in the expedition.

Just as the completion of the work on the field guide at the end of the 1970s resulted in a great increase in artistic activity, at the

New Siberian Islands, July 1994
Foto: Henrik Ekman

beginning of the 1990s Lars Jonsson is again able to concentrate more on his art – work which is interspersed with travels and research. In the ornithological sphere, he completes a major project on divers which is published in 1992, following this with comprehensive studies of large gulls which are still in progress.

The 1990s are devoted largely to artistic work, and he has several exhibitions in Sweden that attract much attention. The Massachusetts Audubon Society invites Lars, as an artist, to contribute pictures for its book *The Nature of Massachusetts*, to be published in association with its centenary year in 1997. Lars spends some time there in autumn 1994 and spring 1995, engaged in painting. An interest in American nature and participation in various exhibitions, including at The National Gallery of Wildlife Art in Wyoming, results in almost annual trips to America. He also travels to India in 1997, along with an international group of wildlife artists within ANF (the Artists for Nature Foundation), in order to paint tigers and other wildlife in central India. The work is presented in a book and in an exhibition at The Burrel Collection in Glasgow in 2000.

The new millennium is greeted by Lars with a new book on Gotland, *Dagrar* [Daylights], which appears in 2000. This comprises passages from the diary and pictures from his later production which reflect the year in his home lands, the cultivated country of southern Gotland.

In 2002 Lars Jonsson reaches his fiftieth year. In May of this year he is appointed as Honorary Doctor of Philosophy at Uppsala University. At the Prins Eugens Waldemarsudde Museum of Art, in Stockholm, a large exhibition of his art is shown, from the earliest works, examples of his illustrations from the books, pages from the sketchbook, and water-colours right up to the most important paintings by the mature artist. It is more and more clear that Lars Jonsson has

not only created a position all of his own in Swedish wildlife-painting, but also influenced the field on an international level. One of the few other Swedish points of comparison is the past master Bruno Liljefors, who for Lars Jonsson still represents an important source of inspiration. During the 1990s, several exhibitions in combination with Liljefors were put together, including, for example, at Kalmar Museum of Art in 1994 and at Örebro Castle in 1997. Lars Jonsson's works suggest an affiliation with tradition at the same time as they clearly show the younger artist's individuality. Or, as the art historian Allan Ellenius writes:

'While fellow-artists in general base their work on the drawing, Jonsson works with the light as the totally crucial factor in the building-up of pictures. The bodies become concentrations of light, sometimes dissolved almost to the point of anonymity – note the point of contact with Liljefors – and integrated into the varied and changeable colour complex of the surroundings. Unity and harmony, a kind of affirmation of a universal harmony, an experience of happiness in everyday life, a world which would rather have the Goshawk resting in the foliage than portray the explosive atttack. The Avocets which are reduced to black-and-white marks among the lagoons' light reflections. Lars Jonsson wrestles with fundamental aesthetic problems, he wishes to preserve the emotional depth of the experience without forswearing himself to the depiction of it. In some water-colours, his preferred medium, the colour seems if anything to be sprinkled on – one expects it to disperse as quickly as the band of mist over the Gotland shoreline. In the dissolution there is the watchful observation which registers the subject's physical appearance in the mind, but also the conviction of the indissoluble relationships which constitute the eternally enigmatic reality.'

BJÖRN LINNELL

Lars after recieving the honorary doctorate at Uppsala University together with Vice–chancellor, professor Bo Sundquist and doctor Anders Wall, honorary member of the University.

ONE-MAN EXHIBITIONS

1968 Naturhistoriska Riksmuseet, Stockholm
1970 Biblioteket i Västerhaninge, Stockholm
Biblioteket i Handen, Stockholm
Gubbängens gymnasium, Stockholm
Gröndalsskolan, Nynäshamn
1972 Galleri Hos Oss, Visby
Karolinska sjukhuset,
Galleri 'Gången', Stockholm
1973 Galleri Z, Odensbacken,Örebro
1976 Galleri Z, Odensbacken, Örebro
1977 Galleri Z, Odensbacken, Örebro
1978 Galleri Z, Odensbacken, Örebro
1979 Forum (Gotlands Konstförening), Visby
1980 *Göran Boström / Lars Jonsson*,
Galleri Z, Odensbacken, Örebro
1981 *Gotland och Spanien i vitt och svart*,
Galleri Händer, Stockholm
1982 *Gunnar Brusewitz Fårö / Lars Jonsson Sudret*,
Konst & Hantverkshuset, Gotland
Lars Jonsson / Jurgen af Rolén,
Galleri W, Simrishamn
1983 *Ön, bilder från en sandrevel*,
Konst & Hantverkshuset, Gotland
Galleri Astley, Uttersberg
Lars Jonsson / Harald Wiberg,
Galleri Z, Odensbacken, Örebro
Naturhistoriska Riksmuseet, Stockholm
Galleri Falbygden, Falköping
1984 *Bird Island* (book release),
Tryon Gallery, London
1985 Börstorps slott, Mariestad
1986 Konst & Hantverkshuset, Gotland
1987 *Bird Reflections*,
Tryon & Moorland Gallery, London
1990 *En dag i maj*,
Konst & Hantverkshuset, Gotland
1992 *Les oiseaux de Lars Jonsson*,
Centre Culturel Suédois, Paris
Galerie Rolf Wahl, Paris
Konstmuseet i Uttersberg, Uttersberg
Fåglar i Europa,
Konst & Hantverkshuset, Gotland
1993 Härnösands Konsthall
(Härnösands Konstförening), Härnösand

Galleri Z, Odensbacken, Örebro
Karlskoga Konsthall
(Karlskoga Konstförening), Karlskoga
1994 *Grafik och skisser*,
Konstnärshuset, Stockholm
Bruno Liljefors / Lars Jonsson,
Kalmar Konstmuseum, Kalmar
1995 *Konstnärer på tundran*,
Naturhistoriska Riksmuseet, Stockholm
Gotlands Konstmuseum, Visby
Galleri S, Östersund
1996 *Björn von Rosen / Lars Jonsson*,
Galleri Kavaletten, Stockholm
Höganäs Museum, Höganäs
The Massachusetts Audubon Society,
Canton, Massachusetts
1997 *Lars Jonsson / Bruno Liljefors*,
Örebro Slott, Örebro
Konst & Hantverkshuset, Gotland
1998 Orangeriet, Linnéträdgården
(Konstsommar i Uppsala), Uppsala
Galleri Z, Odensbacken, Örebro
1999 Galerie de Pierpont (Golf de Pierpont), Brussels
Folkets hus konsthall
(Alvesta Allmänna Konstförening), Alvesta
Dagrar (Millennium-mappen),
Konstmuseet Galleri Astley, Uttersberg
(also shown in Eskilstuna and in Torshälla)
2000 *Dagrar*, Österbybruks Herrgård
(Bruno Liljeforsstiftelsen), Österbybruk
2001 Brunnsta värdshus
(Metallförbundet Volvo), Eskilstuna
(also at ABF, Eskilstuna)
2002 *Fåglar och Ljus*,
Prins Eugens Waldemarsudde, Stockholm
2003 *Fåglar och Ljus*, Kulturcentrum
(Ronneby Kulturförening), Ronneby

GROUP EXHIBITIONS AND CO-EXHIBITIONS

1971 *Liljewalchs vårsalong*,
Liljewalchs Konsthall, Stockholm
Sommarutställning (Gotlands bildningsförbund)
Biblioteket, Burgsvik
Katthamra Gård, Katthamra
Sudersands Badrestaurang, Fårö
Exp. mondiale de la chasse - exposition artistique,
Budapest
1972 *Unga tecknare*,
Nationalmuseet, Stockholm
Fåglar – Vingar – Flykt,
Sveagalleriet, Stockholm
Leva med naturen,
Naturhistoriska Riksmuseet, Stockholm
Naturen som motiv,
Borås Museum, Borås
Naturen som motiv,
Örebro Läns Museum, Örebro
Naturen som motiv,
Skara Teater, Skara
1974 *Naturen som motiv*,
Konsthallen Skellefteå, Skellefteå
Allan Andersson / Gunnar Brusewitz / Lars Jonsson / Harald Wiberg
(Galleri Z), Fiskingegården, Asker, Örebro
1975 *Animals in Art*,
Royal Ontario Museum, Toronto
1976 *Djur i natur*,
Kalmar konstmuseum, Kalmar
1979 *Jubileumsutställning 1969–1979*,
Fiskingegården, Asker, Örebro
1980 *Gunnar Brusewitz / Lars Jonsson / Harald Wiberg*,
Konst & Hantverkshuset, Gotland
Djur och natur, Klippans bibliotek
(Klippans Konstförening), Klippan
1981 *Agneta Engström / Lars Jonsson / Jurgen af Rolén*,
Konst & Hantverkshuset, Gotland
1982 *1982 Bird Art Exhibition*,
LYWAM (Leigh Yawkey Woodson Art
Museum), Wausau, Wisconsin
1983 *Birds in Art Exhibition*,
LYWAM, Wausau, Wisconsin
(travelling exhibition)
Explorers Hall, National Geographic Society,

227

Washington D.C.
Denver Museum of Natural History,
  Denver, Colorado (1984)
Houston Museum of Natural Science,
  Houston, Texas (1984)

1984 Galleri Z, Odensbacken, Örebro
The 1984 Birds in Art Exhibition, LYWAM,
  Wausau, Wisconsin
    (travelling exhibition)
  San Bernadino County Museum,
    Redlands, California
  California Academy of Sciences,
    San Francisco, California
  University of Alaska Museum,
    Fairbanks, Alaska (1985)
  Anchorage Historical and Fine Arts Museum,
    Anchorage, Alaska (1985)
  Alaska State Museum, Juneau, Alaska (1985)
Northern shores, Saga gallery
  (Saga, Scandinavian Art Ltd), London

1985 Galleri Falbygden, Falköping
Inaugural exhibition for Society of Wildlife Art for the
  Nation (SWAN), Guildhall Art Gallery,
  London
Birds in Art 1985, LYWAM,
  Wausau, Wisconsin
    (travelling exhibition)
  Rochester Museum and Science Center,
    Rochester, New York
  Missouri Botanical Garden,
    St Louis, Missouri (1986)
  Springfield Science Museum,
    Springfield, Massachusetts (1986)

1986 *Bevingat*, Konstcentrum, Gävle
Birds in Art 1986, LYWAM,
  Wausau, Wisconsin
    (travelling exhibition)
  Frye Art Museum, Seattle, Washington
  Santa Barbara Museum of Natural History,
    Santa Barbara, California (1987)
  Bernice Pauahi Bishop Museum,
    Honolulu, Hawaii (1987)
  Beijing Natural History Museum,
    Beijing (1987)

1987 *Stockholm Art Fair* (Galleri Astley), Stockholm
Wildlife in Art LYWAM, Wausau, Wisconsin
    (travelling exhibition)
  Cumming Nature Center, Rochester
  Museum & Science Center,
    Naples, New York
  Lakeview Museum of Arts and Sciences,
    Peoria, Illinois
  Huntington Galleries, Huntington,

West Virginia
Cincinnati Museum of Natural History,
  Cincinnati, Ohio
The R.W. Norton Art Gallery,
  Shreveport, Louisiana (1988)
Cumberland Museum and Science,
  Nashville, Tennessee (1988)
Springfield Science Museum,
  Springfield, Massachusetts (1988)
Anniston Museum of Natural History,
  Anniston, Alabama (1988)
Milwaukee Public Museum,
  Milwaukee, Wisconsin (1988)
Gibbes Art Gallery,
  Charleston, South Carolina (1989)
Grafikutställning,
  Konst & Hantverkshuset, Gotland
Birds in Art 1987 LYWAM, Wausau, Wisconsin
    (travelling exhibition)
  Rochester Museum and Science Center,
    Rochester, New York
  Natural History Museum of Los Angeles
    County, Los Angeles, California (1988)
  Field Museum of Natural History,
    Chicago, Illinois (1988)
Björn Dal / Lars Jonsson / Staffan Ullström,
  Galleri Z, Odensbacken, Örebro

1988 *Stockholm Art Fair* (Galleri Astley), Stockholm
Birds in Art 1988 LYWAM, Wausau, Wisconsin
    (travelling exhibition)
  Missouri Botanical Garden,
    St Louis, Missouri (1989)
  Cincinnati Museum of Natural History,
    Cincinnati, Ohio (1989)
  High Desert Museum, Bend, Oregon (1989)

1989 *D'après Nature*,
  La Galerie d'Art Municipale (Des musées de la
    Ville de Luxembourg et le Musée National
    d'Histoire Naturelle), Luxemburg
Stockholm Art Fair (Galleri Astley), Stockholm
Jubileumsutställning 'Dygnet Runt',
  Fiskingegården, Asker, Örebro
Birds in Art 1989,
  LYWAM, Wausau, Wisconsin
    (travelling exhibition)
  Houston Museum of Natural Science,
    Houston, Texas
  Arnot Art Museum,
    Elmira, New York (1990)
  Anchorage Museum of History and Art,
    Anchorage, Alaska (1990)
  Patrick & Beatrice Haggerty Museum of Art,
    Milwaukee, Wisconsin (1990)

Grafikutställning, Galleri S, Östersund
1990 *Rovfåglar*,
  Nationalmuseet, Stockholm
  Naturhistoriska Riksmuseet, Stockholm
  Riksutställningar, Uppsala universitet,
    Lövsta herrgård, Lövstabruk
Stockholm Art Fair (Galleri Astley), Stockholm
Jubileum–Galleriet 10 år,
  Konst & Hantverkshuset, Gotland
Birds in Art 1990,
  LYWAM, Wausau, Wisconsin
    (travelling exhibition)
  High Desert Museum, Bend, Oregon
  Fine Arts Museum of the South,
    Mobile, Alabama (1991)
  Rochester Museum and Science Center,
    Rochester, New York (1991)
  Wendell Gilley Museum,
    Southwest Harbor, Maine (1991)

1991 *Stockholm Art Fair* (Galleri Astley), Stockholm
Luft, Ängvards salong, Vamlingbo, Gotland
28th Annual Exhibition, *Society of Wildlife Artists*,
  Mall Galleries, London
Birds in Art 1991,
  LYWAM, Wausau, Wisconsin
    (travelling exhibition)
  American Museum of Natural History,
    New York
  Ward Museum of Wildfowl Art,
    Salisbury, Maryland (1992)
  Washington State Historical Society,
    Tacoma, Washington (1992)

1992 *Stockholm Art Fair* (Galleri Astley), Stockholm
Djur och Natur i Konsten, Galleri Linné, Sala
Drawn from life, Wildlife Art Gallery,
  Lavenham, Suffolk
Birds in Art 1992,
  LYWAM, Wausau, Wisconsin
    (travelling exhibition)
  Buffalo Museum of Science,
    Buffalo, New York
  Carnegie Museum of Natural History,
    Pittsburgh, Pennsylvania (1993)
  High Desert Museum, Bend, Oregon (1993)
Art and the Animal, (Society of Animal Artists),
  Roger Tory Peterson Institute of Natural
    History, Jamestown, New York
    (travelling exhibition)
  R. W. Norton Art Gallery,
    Shreveport, Louisiana
  Oklahoma Museum of Natural History,
    Norman, Oklahoma
  Oshkosh Public Museum, Oshkosh,

Wisconsin (1993)

Houston Museum of Natural Science,
Houston, Texas (1993)

1993 *Stockholm Art Fair* (Galleri Astley), Stockholm

Djur och Natur i Konsten, Galleri Linné, Sala

30th Annual Exhibition, Society of Wildlife Artists,
Mall Galleries, London

Birds in Art 1993,
LYWAM, Wausau, Wisconsin
(travelling exhibition)

New Mexico Museum of Natural History and
Science, Albuquerque, New Mexico

Dayton Museum of Natural History,
Dayton, Ohio (1994)

Museum of the Rockies,
Bozeman, Montana (1994)

1994 *Djur och Natur i Konsten*, Galleri Linné, Sala

Birds in Art 1994,
LYWAM, Wausau, Wisconsin
(travelling exhibition)

Naturhistoriska Riksmuseet, Stockholm

Hunter Museum of Art, Chattanooga,
Tennessee (1995)

Under fågelsträcket, Falsterbo Konsthall, Falsterbo

1995 *Djur och Natur i Konsten*, Galleri Linné, Sala

The flight of the Cranes,
ANF in Extremadura, Zeist Castle, Zeist
(travelling exhibition)

Museo de Cirencias-Naturalis, Madrid

Claustro Garcia-Matos, Caceres

Centro Cultural Iglesias De San Francisco,
Trujillo (1996)

Wildlife Art Gallery, Lavenham (1996)

LYWAM, Wausau, Wisconsin (1997)

Wildlife Art, Christie's, South Kensington
(in association with WWF), London

Birds in Art 1995,
LYWAM, Wausau, Wisconsin
(travelling exhibition)

Waterfowl Festival Inc.,
Easton Maryland

Wendell Gilley Museum,
Southwest Harbor, Maine (1996)

A brush with nature
(Wildfowl & Wetlands Trust, Slimbridge),
Painswick House, Gloucestershire

1996 *Djur och Natur i Konsten*, Galleri Linné, Sala

Birds in Art 1996,
LYWAM, Wausau, Wisconsin
(travelling exhibition)

Dayton Museum of Natural History,
Dayton, Ohio

James Ford Bell Museum of Natural History,

Minneapolis (1997)

National Museum of Wildlife Art,
Jackson, Wyoming (1997)

Samtida konstnärer ser på Liljefors,
Prins Eugens Waldemarsudde, Stockholm

1997 *Wonders of Nature – World of Wildlife Art*
(Mondiale Fine Arts), National Gallery,
Colombo

Wonders of Nature – Hunters in the Wild
(Mondiale Fine Arts), Holiday Inn,
Crowne Plaza, Dubai

Djur och Natur i Konsten, Galleri Linné, Sala

Birds in Art 1997,
LYWAM, Wausau, Wisconsin
(travelling exhibition)

Lakeview Museum of Arts and Sciences,
Peoria, Illinois (1998)

Michelson Museum of Art,
Marshall, Texas (1998)

1998 *Djur och Natur i Konsten*, Galleri Linné, Sala

Birds in Art 1998,
LYWAM, Wausau, Wisconsin
(travelling exhibition)

Museum of the Southwest,
Midland, Texas (1999)

Lindsay Wildlife Museum,
Walnut Creek, California (1999)

Delaware Museum of Natural History,
Wilmington, Delaware (1999)

1999 *Djur och Natur i Konsten*, Galleri Linné, Sala

Western Visions,
National Museum of Wildlife Art,
Jackson Hole, Wyoming

Birds in Art 1999,
LYWAM, Wausau, Wisconsin
(travelling exhibition)

Saginaw Art Museum,
Saginaw, Michigan (2000)

Wendell Gilley Museum,
Southwest Harbor, Maine (2000)

Michelson Museum of Art,
Marshall, Texas (2000)

Eco Art Exhibition (Taipei Eco Art Association),
National Museum of History, Taipei

2000 *Wild Tigers of Bandhavgarh* (ANF in India),
Burrell Collection, Glasgow
(travelling exhibition)

Zeist Castle, Zeist (2001)

Frankfurt ZOO, Frankfurt (2002)

Djur och Natur i Konsten , Galleri Linné, Sala

Wildlife Art for a New Century,
National Museum of Wildlife Art,
Jacksonhole, Wyoming

Birds in Art 2000,
LYWAM Wausau, Wisconsin

Western Visions,
National Museum of Wildlife Art,
Jackson Hole, Wyoming

2001 *Animali nell'Arte,*
Museo Civico di Zoologia, Rome

Djur och Natur i Konsten, Galleri Linné, Sala

Contemporary Naturalism,
Gerald Peters Gallery, Santa Fe, Arizona

Konst på båtarna
(Kulturcentralen Ars Gotlandica),
Galleri Ars Gotlandica, MS Visby,

Birds in Art 2001,
LYWAM, Wausau, Wisconsin
(travelling exhibition)

Kennedy Museum of Art,
Ohio University, Athens, Ohio

String Room Gallery,
Wells College Aurora, New York (2002)

Linsay Wildlife Museum,
Walnut Creek, California (2002)

Western Visions,
National Museum of Wildlife Art,
Jackson Hole, Wyoming

2002 *Djur och Natur i Konsten*, Galleri Linné, Sala

Western Visions,
National Museum of Wildlife Art,
Jackson Hole, Wyoming

Birds in Art 2002,
LYWAM Wausau, Wisconsin

Nature's Legacy: Wildlife and Wild Country
(Sierra Club), J. N. Bartfield Gallery,
New York City

Wildlife and the Artists,
Wildlife Art Gallery, Lavenham

Represented

Leigh Yawkey Woodson Art Museum,
Wausau, Wisconsin

The Massachusetts Audubon Society,
Canton, Massachusetts.

Miljödepartementet, Regeringskansliet,
Stockholm

National Museum of Wildlife Art,
Jacksonhole, Wyoming

Naturhistoriska Riksmuseet, Stockholm

Uppsala universitet, Uppsala

State art council and in several local councils and
authorities in Sweden

BIBLIOGRAPHY

BOOKS

Fåglar i naturen. Skog, park, trädgård. Wahlström &
Widstrand, Stockholm, 1976
Fugler i naturen. Skog, park og hage. Cappelen, Oslo, 1977
Fugle i naturen. Skov, park og have. Gyldendal,
Copenhagen, 1977
Linnut luonnossa. Metsä, puisto ja puutarha.
Tammi, Helsinki, 1977
Birds of wood, park and garden.
Penguin Books, Harmondsworth, 1978
Vögel in Wald, Park und Garten. Franckh, Stuttgart, 1977
Vogels in hun eigen omgeving. Tuin en park.
B.V. W. J. Thieme & Cie, Zutphen, 1977
Os Pássaros. Bosques, parques e jaruins.
Círculo de Leitores, Cacém, 1977/78

Fåglar i naturen. Hav och kust.
Wahlström & Widstrand, Stockholm, 1976
Fugler i naturen. Hav og kyst. Cappelen, Oslo, 1977
Fugle i naturen. Hav og kyst. Gyldendal, Copenhagen, 1977
Linnut luonnossa. Meri ja rannikko.
Tammi, Helsinki, 1977
Birds of sea and coast.
Penguin Books, Harmondsworth, 1978
Die Vögel der Meeresküste. Franckh, Stuttgart, 1977
Vogels in hun eigen omgeving. Wad en kust.
B.V. W. J. Thieme & Cie, Zutphen, 1977

Fåglar i naturen. Sjö, å, träsk och åkermark.
Wahlström & Widstrand, Stockholm, 1977
Fugler i naturen. Åker, vann og våtmark.
Cappelen, Oslo, 1978
Fugle i naturen. So og å, mose og mark.
Gyldendal, Copenhagen, 1978
Linnut luonnossa. Järvet, joet, suot ja peltoaukeat.
Tammi, Helsinki, 1978
Birds of lake, river, marsh and field.
Penguin Books, Harmondsworth, 1978
Vögel der Fluren und am Wasser. Franckh, Stuttgart, 1978
Vogels in hun eigen omgeving. Zoetwater, moerassen en veld.
B.V. W. J. Thieme & Cie, Zutphen, 1977
Os Pássaros. Lagos, rios e campos.
Círculo de Leitores, Cacém, 1977/78
Fåglar i naturen. Fjäll och skogsland.
Wahlström & Widstrand, Stockholm, 1978

Fugler i naturen. Fjell og barskog. Cappelens, Oslo, 1979
Fugle i naturen. Fjeld og fjeldskov.
Gyldendal, Copenhagen, 1979
Linnut luonnossa. Tunturit ja havumetsä.
Tammi, Helsinki, 1979
Birds of mountain regions.
Penguin Books, Harmondsworth, 1979
Vogels in hun eigen omgeving. Bos, weide en fjeld.
B.V. W. J. Thieme & Cie, Zutphen, 1979

Fåglar i naturen. Medelhavsländerna och alperna.
Wahlström & Widstrand, Stockholm, 1980
Fugle i Middelhavslandene og Alperne.
Gyldendal, Copenhagen, 1982
Birds of the Mediterranean and Alps.
Croom Helm, London, 1982
Vogels in hun eigen omgeving. Alpen en Middellandse. B.V.
W. J. Thieme & Cie, Zutphen, 1982
Linnut luonnossa. Välimeri ja Alpit.
Tammi, Helsinki, 1983

Ön, bilder från en sandrevel. Atlantis, Stockholm 1983
Bird Island, pictures from a shoal of sand.
Croom Helm, London, 1984
Lintusaaren elämää. Weilin+Göös, Espoo, 1988

En dag i maj. Atlantis, Stockholm, 1990

Fåglar i Europa med Nordafrika och Mellanöstern.
Wahlström & Widstrand, Stockholm, 1992
Birds of Europe with North Africa and the Middle East.
Christopher Helm, London, 1992
Die Vögel Europas und des Mittelmeerraumes.
Franckh-Kosmos, Stuttgart, 1992
Birds of Europe with North Africa and the Middle East.
Princeton University Press, Princeton, 1993
Vogels van Europa. Noord-Afrika en het Midden-Oosten.
Tirion, Baarn, 1993
Fugler. Europa·Nord-Afrika·Midtosten.
Cappelen, Oslo, 1994
Fugle i Europa med Nordafrika og Mellemosten.
Gyldendal, Copenhagen, 1994
Euroopan orolf. Eurooppa, Pohjois-Afrikka ja Lähi-itä.
Tammi, Helsinki, 1994
Les Oiseaux d'Europe, d'Afrique du Nord et du Moyen-Orient.
Nathan, Paris, 1994

Aves de Europa con el Norte de África y el Próximo Oriente.
Ediciones Omega, Barcelona, 1994
Ocells d'Europa amb el Nord d'Àfrica i l'Orient Mitjà.
Edicions Omega, Barcelona, 1994
Ptaki Europy. I Obszaru `Sròdziemnomorskiego.
Muza, Warszawa, 1998
*Euroopa Linnud. Euroopa, Põhja-Aafrika ja Lähis-Ida orolf
välimääraja.* Eesti Entsüklopeediakirjastus,
Tallin, 2000
Lommar (with Torulf Tysse).
Sveriges Ornitologiska Förening, Stockholm, 1992

Dagrar. Wahlström & Widstrand, Stockholm, 2000

The Nature of Massachusetts (illustrations; text by C.
Leahy, J. H. Mitchell and T. Conuel). Addison-
Wesley, Reading, 1996

ESSAYS AND FOREWORDS

'Att måla', 'Arbetssätt' and other texts in: *Katalog till
utställning på Naturhistoriska Riksmuseet,*
Stockholm, 1984
Foreword in: Martha Hill, *Bruno Liljefors, mästarens blick,*
Norstedts, Stockholm, 1987
'Bruno Liljefors' impact on swedish painters' in:
Wildlife and Art (conference abstracts),
University of Minnesota, Minneapolis-St Paul,
1988
'Dinosaurier kan flyga' in: exhibition catalogue at
Konstmuseet Galleri Astley in Uttersberg, 1992
'Vem upptäckte räven' in: *Samtida konstnärer ser på
Liljefors* (katalog 39: 96). Prins Eugens
Waldemarsudde, Stockholm, 1997
'Atelje i det fria' in: Hans Henrik Brummer and Allan
Ellenius (eds.), *Naturen som livsrum. Ekologiska
perspektiv i modärn litteratur och bildkonst, Natur och
Kultur,* Stockholm, 1998
Foreword in: Todd Wilkinson and Kent Ullberg,
Monuments to Nature, International Graphics,
Scottsdale, Arizona, 1998

Articles in popular scientific magazines and periodical journals

'Fågelvår på Öja'. *Fauna och Flora* Nr 3, 1971

'Några fågeldagar i Niger'. *Fauna och Flora* Nr 3, 1972

'Vadarkaraktärer'. *Fåglar i Stockholmstrakten* (Stockholms ornitologiska förening), Nr 2, 1973

'Rovfåglar vid Bosporen'. *Fåglar i Stockholmstrakten* Nr 1, 1973

'Gotländsk fågelstrand'. *Gotlands turisten*, 1975

'Aftonfalken på Gotland sommaren 1976'. *Bläcku* (Gotlands ornitologiska förenings tidskrift), Nr 2, 1976

'Fågelbordet och dess gäster' (Lars Jonsson and Per Göran Bentz). *Bläcku* Nr 2, 1977

'Sjunde januari 1980'. *Fältbiologen* Nr 1, 1980

'Identification of stints and peeps' (Peter Grant and Lars Jonsson). *British Birds* Nr 7, 1984

'Fältbestämning av små Calidris-vadare'. *Vår Fågelvärld* Nr 5, 1984

'Field identification of smaller sandpipers within the genus *Calidris*' (Lars Jonsson and Rickard V. Veit). *American Birds* Nr 5, 1984

'Liten havsfågelbok'. *Bläcku* Nr 1, 1986

'Liten havsfågelbok, 2: Dvärgmås och tretåig mås'. *Bläcku* Nr 2, 1986

'Bird on an island'. *Defenders*, May/June 1987

'Ett ord från den slumrande Homeros'. *Anser* Nr 1, 1994

'Bergänder och viggar'. *Fågelåret 1994*, supplement to *Vår Fågelvärld* Nr 22, 1995

'The image of a bird'. *Birds*, RSPB's magazine, Nr 5, spring 1993

'Gulfotade trutar'. *Vår Fågelvärld* (Sveriges ornitologiska förening) Nr 8, 1996

'Splitting, nya arter för landet och bestämning per fax'. *Fågelåret 1995*, supplement to *Vår Fågelvärld* Nr 2, 1996

'Baltic Lesser Black-backed Gull *Larus fuscus fuscus* – moult, ageing and identification'. *Birding World* Nr 8, 1998

'Yellow-legged gulls and yellow-legged Herring Gulls in the Baltic'. *Alula* Nr 3, 1998

'Genetic Diversity in Arctic Lemmigs' (K. Fredga, V. Feodorov, G. Jarrell and L. Jonsson). *Ambio* Nr 3, 1999

'American Herring Gulls at Niagara Falls and Newfoundland' (with Bruce Mactavish). *Birders Journal* Nr 2, 2001

Books with pictures by and text on Lars Jonsson

Brynildson, Inga, and Hagge, Woody. *Birds in Art, The Masters*. Leigh Yawkey Woodson Art Museum, Wausau and Konecky & Konecky, New York, 1990

Busby, John. *Drawing Birds*. The Royal Society for the Protection of Birds, Sandy, 1986

Edman, S. 'En skånsk resa' in *1996 Skåne*, Svenska Turistföreningen, Uppsala, 1995

Hammond, Nicholas (ed.). *Artists for Nature in Extremadura*. The Wildlife Art Gallery, Lavenham, 1995

Hammond, Nicholas (ed.). *Tigers. Artists for Nature in India*. The Wildlife Art Gallery, Lavenham, 2000

Hammond, Nicholas. *Twentieth Century Wildlife Artists*. Croom Helm Ltd, Beckenham, and The Overlook Press, New York, 1986

Jonsson, H. B., Broberg, G., and Johannesson, L. (eds.). *Historiens vingslag* (picture facing page 33), Stockholm, 1987

Myers, J. P. '*Making sense of sexual nonsense*'. In Audubon Nature Yearbook 1991, New York, 1991

Pasquier, Roger F., and Farrand, John Jr. *Masterpieces of Bird Art: 700 Years of Ornithological Illustration*. Abbeville Press, New York, 1991

Rayfield, Susan. *Wildlife painting techniques of modern masters*. Watson-Guptill Publications, New York, 1985

Shillcock, Robin D'Arcy. *Pintores de la Naturaleza*. Banco Central Hispano and SEO/Birdlife, Madrid, 1997

Catalogue texts and articles on Lars Jonsson (selection)

Brusewitz, Gunnar. 'Fågelmålare i storformat' in: *Julstämning* 1989

Davis, Tom. 'Mirrors to the soul: the art of Lars Jonsson; in: *Wildlife Art News*, May/June 1990

Ellenius, Allan. 'Fågelbilder förr och nu' in: *Lars Jonsson* (katalog), Naturhistoriska Riksmuseet, Stockholm, 1984

Ellenius, Allan. 'Lars Jonsson' in: Lars Jonsson and Bruno Liljefors (katalog), *Örebro slott*, 1997

Hedengren, Uriel. 'Lars Jonsson, en man med många penslar i elden' in: *På Linjen* Nr 1, 1995

Hill, Martha. 'Lars Jonsson: A life in the field'. *Living Bird*, Winter 2000

Hillker, Li. 'Lasse och hans fåglar'. *Vi Nr* 20, 1979

Holmberg, Lars. 'Det är ju otroligt vad den pojken kan!'. *Expressen*, 24 februari 1968

Houkjaer, Niels. 'Fuglemanden'. *Berlingske Tidende*, 23 §juli 2000

Hård, Calle. 'Höken som fångar skönheten i flykten'. *Expressen*, 23 september 1984

Karlsson, Lars-Ingemar. 'Gotländsk fågelmålare fångar längtan till frihet'. *Dagens Nyheter*, 30 oktober 1989

Lagerkvist, Bengt. 'Fångad i Flykten'. In exhibition catalogue: Lars Jonsson – Bruno Liljefors, Kalmar Konstmuseum, 1994

Lack, David M. 'Lars Jonsson, an introduction'. In text i catalogue for exhibition 'Lars Jonsson Bird Reflections', Tryon & Moorland Gallery, London, 1987

Lind, Ingela. Text in catalogue for exhibition at Gotlands Konstmuseum, Visby, 1995

Linnell, Björn (ed.). 'Lars Jonsson'. *Ord & bild*, 1985

Moberg, Ulf Thomas. 'Lars Jonsson'. Text i catalogue for exhibition at Galérie de Pierpont, Brussels, 1999

Montan, Ulla, and Rasmusson, Ludvig. *Svenska profiles*, Svenska institutet, Stockholm, 1999

Peterson, Roger Tory. 'A letter to Lars Jonsson'. *Bird Watcher's Digest*, July/August 1984

Storm, Ingvar. 'Bevingade bilder'. *Upp & Ner* Nr 12/1990–1/1991

Wiking, Peter. 'Lars Jonsson – fågelmålare'. *Sveriges Natur* Nr 1, 1984

William-Olsson, Margareta. 'Fåglarnas oförtröttliga utforskare'. *Göteborgs-posten*, 23 mars 1997

Film

'Ögonblick vid stranden, en film om konstnären Lars Jonsson' by Rainer Hartleb (director) and Staffan Lindqvist (photography), Olympia filmproduktion HB, Stockholm, 1998

Postscript

This book began as a future project, a beginning of something new in which new paintings not yet done would form the core. Perhaps it has instead become a pause in our steps – a reflection about the moment and what has been. Over the years loose ideas and proposals have been brought up from different quarters concerning a book on and about my pictures, but these seeds have never landed in the right soil. When the possibility arose to exhibit at Prins Eugens Waldemarsudde in Stockholm around the time of the start of the new millennium, such a book project suddenly acquired a concrete framework, in time and space. The exhibition was fixed for October 2002, almost three years ahead. Now the future as then was is to some extent to look in the driving mirror, and I can only confirm that the journey into something new became as much a journey back and into time. It was just as much reflections over the 45 years which have passed since I did my first bird drawing as the aspiration to say something new. During the last two years I have now and then felt frustrated and disappointed that I have not managed to paint more than I have done. The book in itself has come to take too much time away from painting, and it seems as if my future project – the new pictures – has barely started. But maybe one has sometimes to sit down and sum up things, compose oneself, in order to take a further step forwards. That's just sour grapes ['Sour said the fox of the rowanberries', as the Swedish fable goes when the fox in disappointment could not reach the delicious red berries].

It probably feels almost better still now when all those paintings remain to be done. Artistic activity cannot be forecast, so neither can mine. But the birds still fly through my inner spirit, and so long as they return to my shore or some other shore in the world I shall happily tell more about them.

Life is what goes on while we are busy doing other things Lennart Hagerfors has prosaically declared, originally a John Lennon quotation. While for a great part of the day I have painted, written and in various ways been occupied with this book – life has gone on; in the form of a love, joy and everyday duty which I have and experience together with Ragnhild and our children Martin, Viktor, Rebecka and Matilda. The life which goes on but which I am not really able to express in my pictures – I am of course occupied with other things. I am very grateful for the long-suffering forbearance of my family.

There are many people who have contributed in various ways to this book's coming to fruition and whom I wish to thank: Björn Linnell for our close collaboration over discussions and his advice in various contexts; Staffan Söderblom for his important contribution and all stimulating discussions; Christer Jonson for his exceptional feel for design when we created the external design of this book; Lennart Rolf of the publishers, Atlantis bokförlag. Magnus Persson has photographed most of the works and the sketchbooks. I wish also to thank Veronica Båtelsson, who alongside Ragnhild attends to much of the practical work in the studio and the business side in general. Henrik Dahl and Per-Arne Wahlgren have got the computers to work when the latter and I were not talking the same language. Finally, I wish to thank Anders Wall and the Beijer Foundation for supporting this book and exhibition in various ways. My thanks also to Hans Henrik Brummer and Göran Söderlund at Waldemarsudde.

Hamra, June 2002